D1452658

CONTINUE IN

HOPE

CONTINUE IN
HOPE

Only God can heal a broken heart

SHIRLEY NOELANI GAMBILL-DE REGO

XULON PRESS

Xulon Press
2301 Lucien Way #415
Maitland, FL 32751
407.339.4217
www.xulonpress.com

Foreword by: Rick Nagaoka Senior Pastor New Hope Waikoloa Church and
Billy Mitchell Senior Pastor Mana Christian Ohana

Due to the changing nature of the Internet, if there are any web addresses, links, or
URLs included in this manuscript, these may have been altered and may no longer
be accessible. The views and opinions shared in this book belong solely to the author
and do not necessarily reflect those of the publisher. The publisher therefore disclaims
responsibility for the views or opinions expressed within the work.

Unless otherwise indicated, Scripture quotations taken from the Holy Bible, New
International Version (NIV). Copyright © 1973, 1978, 1984, 2011 by Biblica, Inc.™.
Used by permission. All rights reserved.

Paperback ISBN-13: 978-1-66287-010-1
Ebook ISBN-13: 978-1-66287-011-8

Continue in Hope

(Ho'omau Mana'olana)

Ho'omau–is the Hawaiian value of perseverance and persistence. In practicing this value, we become more tenacious and resilient, and thus, more courageous.

Ho'omau–also means to perpetuate, and to continue in a way that causes good to be long-lasting.

Mana'olana–Hope, confidence, expectation; to hope.

Dedication Page

To my granddaughter Hualilia'omalie Gambill your life will be different from that of mine. Better, with the love and grace of God, for I prayed for you, and God who hears from heaven is faithful to answer. You will always be "My Love"

Alexander and Duke, the older I get the closer I get to you. Thank you, Jesus, for eternal life.

Table of Contents

Foreword

My connection with Shirley De Rego began almost fifteen years ago. In that time, I have journeyed alongside her through some challenging life experiences. I remember early on after hearing her testimony for the first time, I sat speechless that even through all the pain and loss that she endured her faith just grew stronger. I've told many that she is a modern-day Job with all that she has faced and overcome, her confidence in the goodness of God remains.

"Though he slay me, yet will I trust (hope) in him" ~ Job 13:15

In my life of ministry, I've witnessed many turn away from God when faced with similar or lesser struggles. She is clear that her faith in God is what has sustained her through it all. It was several years back that I encouraged Shirley to write a book because more people needed to hear her story. So, to this may I say that I am beyond honored to write the forward for her book, "Continue in Hope".

At some point in our lives, we will all face some type of adversity, it's how you walk through them that will determine how you stand on the other side. When you think you've reached the end of your rope; I hope that Shirley's story will inspire you to continue in hope.

If you know Shirley, it's sometimes hard to keep track of what she is doing next. Whether it's running the Alex & Duke De Rego Foundation, partnering with the young lifeguard program, working in the mortgage lending industry, serving in her church or helping those in need, Shirley's actions will always put others first. This book is just another way to help someone, perhaps like yourself through a dark time in your life and remind you that there is hope.

I will leave you with a quote from another woman who had unwavering faith in the midst of adversity.

"This is what the past is for! Every experience God gives us, every person He puts in our lives are the perfect preparation for the future that only He can see." — Corrie Ten Boom, The Hiding Place

May this book bless and encourage you as it has me,
Rick Nagaoka
Senior Pastor
New Hope Waikoloa, Waikoloa, Hawai'i Island

Foreword

"Shirley"

Finally, the book has been written of such excruciating hurt and supernatural healing. The true story that is revealed in this book will encourage you to turn to the living God in your darkest moments! My sister, Shirley, has found a joy through her testing that only God could ever bring! Check it out!

Kahu Billy Mitchell, Senior Pastor
Mana Christian Ohana, Waimea, Hawai'i Island

Chapter 1:

Hawaiian Roots

A rescue helicopter passed over the truck; circling the sky in front of us; their spotlights scanning the ocean waters below. My heart raced as if it would beat right out of my chest. I looked at the clock on the dash, 9:20PM; we had completed what would have been an hour and twenty-minute drive in forty-five minutes. My husband Lamar had been speeding all the way but that was of little concern to me. I looked around, unfamiliar with this side of the island, the darkness seemed to add to the disorientation.

Just past Konawena High School, we took a side road off the main highway. One of the local fishermen was waiting for us and we were now following him down the dark mountainside road through bushes and trees. Lamar followed closely behind him careful not to leave the trail.

"Please, please, God, let them find him." my ten-year-old son cried out in the backseat as our truck skid down the mountainside.

A clearing opened before us revealing an ambulance. I stared in disbelief as the spotlight from the helicopter danced across the water. Was I watching a movie? Maybe it was a bad dream I would soon wake up from. "Please, Father," I prayed, barely above a whisper, "let Alexander be okay."

One of my mother's famous sayings was, "Shirley, God will never give you more than you can handle."

I tried my best to hang on to her words of encouragement despite what life threw at me but I couldn't help feeling that maybe God was delivering things to the wrong Shirley. Year after year, tragedy after tragedy, I began to doubt if there was much more I could handle. The interesting thing about God is how he really does know how much we can take. Later in life, I found the scripture my mother, and many others, often misquoted,

"No temptation has overtaken you except what is common to mankind. And God is faithful; he will not let you be tempted beyond what you can bear. But when you are tempted, he will also provide a way out so that you can endure it." *1 Corinthians 10:13 NIV*

"...he will also provide a way out so that you can endure it." To me, those were the words which solidified it all. Never, ever, would I have been able to endure all that I have on my own. The only reason I did not find myself numbed out on drugs or in a drunken stupor to dull the pain was because I knew God would get me through each of these heart-wrenching trials. I didn't know how he would do it but if I had that kind of certainty, I would not have been able to call it faith.

We can never see it when we are younger, but as we grow older, it becomes evident the pieces God puts into place long before an event happens. In my case, God knew what he was doing when he made Rosalie Kamila Akau my mother. The Bible says "He knew me before He placed me in my mother's womb". (Jeremiah 1:5) I am blessed that she was my mom. A lot of my strength came from my mother; strength she received from the Lord.

She was born on August 9, 1938 the oldest of ten children; daughter of Alexander Akau and Mary Ako. My grandparents had Hawaiian and Chinese heritage. I never met my grandfather but living on the Big Island of Hawaii, Waimea, it was next to impossible to forget him. Waimea is a small ranch town; everyone knows each other. The old timers knew exactly which family you belonged to; mine being the Akau family. The green hillsides are scattered with cattle, forest trails, hidden waterfalls, expensive homes and deep cowboy history. I realize most people don't picture cowboys when they think of Hawaii but ranching is the heritage of Waimea. Growing up here it wasn't unusual seeing cowboys riding their horses to the local bank and store. Even though it is now a thing of the past, there are still historical pictures in some of the stores and banks to remind us of our heritage. A few of those pictures include my grandfather, Alexander Akau.

Early in Mommy's life, she experienced the loss of three sisters—one was still born, another died in her crib, and another from whooping cough. Although the memories of their deaths were vague since she too was a little girl, I'm sure they factored in to the person she became. Her parents did not have a lot of money, my grandfather was a cowboy for Kahua Ranch and grandma was a homemaker. They were given an old army cargo truck which they used as the family's means of transportation. My siblings and I would laugh at her telling stories of my grandfather driving them to see family, or to a church service, in this vehicle.

Since she was the oldest, she often did many things a son would normally do for the family. She went hunting, fishing and diving for long hours with her father to help feed the family. She was also responsible for helping to care for her four sisters and two brothers. Many nights after a long day at work my grandfather would come home drunk. Grandma, afraid he would start to pick on the kids, had Mommy pack up the younger kids and take them to hide in the kiawe trees. Even though she could hear him fighting with her mother, there was nothing she could do but stay where she was with her siblings until their father fell asleep. My mother had such deep respect for my grandmother and cried many times after her death. Life is interesting in that way as I now experience the same feelings for her.

From the stories she told, I knew my grandfather was a very strict man. One of the happiest times of her life was when her father agreed to let her go to a girls' school in Kohala. Because of the distance between school and home she was able to live and board at the school. Although she loved her new freedom, she never stopped worrying about her mother, sisters, or brothers.

Mommy was very close with her siblings and they often helped each other; a quality that passed on to me, my siblings, and our cousins. She lived and grew up near the ocean, in one of the most beautiful places on the Big Island, Kawaihae. From the patio you could see the beautiful Pacific Ocean and watch dolphins and whales perform. It was no wonder why Mommy always loved her Kawaihae. I have fond memories of my grandparents' home, running around their patio as a young girl on the weekends with my cousins as Mommy ate, sang songs, and drank Olympia beer with her brothers and sisters. One big family—always.

My father was in the Navy and Mommy was living in Oahu working as a housekeeper for the Fairbank Family in Ainahina. They met each other and later married on December 16, 1957. Soon after they married, my father was relocated to San Diego,

California and then to Oakland, California. Mommy returned to the Big Island in 1959 to see her father who had been diagnosed with lung cancer and was ill. She was pregnant with my older brother, Bronson, and stayed on the Big Island until after he was born in July.

She returned to Oakland only to turn around and fly back to the Big Island a few months later for my grandfather's funeral. My sister, Lana, and I were born in Oakland and my youngest brother, Randy, was born in San Diego. By this time, my father's enrollment time in the Navy had come to an end. So, in 1964, we moved to the Big Island. My parents had their own businesses; my father owned and operated Rose's Taxi and Mommy was an independent contractor delivering mail in the Kawaihae area as there were no post office in those days. Bronson, Lana, and I would go with her to deliver the mail because she was afraid of lizards and didn't like opening the mailboxes. In fact, all of Mommy's brothers and sisters have been afraid of lizards. I have never figured out why.

My parents also operated a laundry service. Mauna Kea Beach Hotel was their primary account. Mommy would pick up the laundry from the hotel and take it to Kona for cleaning. My sister and I loved accompanying her on these trips; we played the whole way to Kona in the back of the van, bouncing around on the pile of dirty laundry. My father also did radio commercial spots for Sure Save Super Market, he was known as "Sam the Sure Save Man". These spots on the radio eventually lead to weekend work at a local radio station in Hilo; he had a voice that was meant for radio. While enlisted in the Navy, he was the radio announcer at Midway; known as "Squeakin' Deacon".

We always had dinner as a family, I remember that being important to my dad. When we were done eating, we would ask to be excused from the table and my dad would determine if we could be excused based on whether or not we had cleaned our plate. My sister Lana spent many nights sitting at the table with our father; she always had a hard time eating all her food. Green peas were the hardest for me.

Because of my father's military background, we were taught to answer our parents with "yes, sir" or "no, sir" as well as "yes, ma'am" and "no, ma'am". Even though my father was strict, I knew he loved me. My parents were very different in their matter of discipline. Mommy was old school—hit first, talk later—but my dad would tell us why were we being disciplined; he would explain everything before you got the belt.

Mommy's family was always around. Two of her sisters—Aggie and Pinki—lived on the same street as us and my uncle Maitland lived with us before getting married and moving into the house next door. Family was always around and I imagined I would have a house full of family, just like Mommy, when I grew up. Things don't always work out the way we plan.

My father met a woman during his weekend job at the radio station in Hilo. He moved out and fathered a child with her. He was offered a job as a radio announcer for KDEO Country radio Station in Waipahu, Oahu. By this time, my parents had been separated for almost a year. My father's relationship with the girlfriend was not working out and he begged my mother for another chance. I was nine years old when Mommy moved us from Waimea to Waipahu. I'm sure this move must have been a combination of still loving my father and trying to keep our family together. I know the move was nothing like what Mommy had expected.

Moving from a small town to the big city was a culture shock for all of us. Our mother's family was all we had ever known growing up. Here we were with no aunties, uncles, or cousins; we didn't know anybody and since we moved during the summer, we didn't have any friends either. The girlfriend my father had broken up with, had found out we were coming and refused to leave the house. So, we found ourselves living at the Pagado Hotel for a month. When she did finally leave the house, she took everything with her. Mommy was devasted, she gave up everything to follow my father who lied to her. She became so overcome with grief, she attempted to take her life by overdosing on pills. I remember crying by the front door as they loaded her onto the ambulance. My parents finally separated for good, a few months before my dad eventually filed for divorce. For a short time after the divorce, she sent us back to Waimea, Bronson lived with Aunty Aggie while Lana and I stayed with Uncle Maitland. Randy was the youngest so he stayed with Mommy. We stayed there until Bronson was injured in a car accident with our cousin; that is when she took us back to Waipahu.

Although my parent's marriage didn't last, my father remained faithful in fulfilling his role as a father. While the required child support back then was only $50 per child, he would pay $125 per child. He also paid the rent on the house and took us grocery shopping once a month. When our father left us, we were devasted. None of us could figure out why Mommy wouldn't move us back to Waimea. When I got older, Mommy told me she could not return and face her family. They had warned her not to follow my dad and when she decided to leave, they had been angry with her. As is the case with most family feuds, their anger didn't last very long. Her youngest brother, Maitland Akau, and his family soon moved to Waipahu with us. Her brother, Alexander Akau, was stationed at Schofield Barracks and her sister Haunani and brother-in-law were stationed at Barbers Point. Almost every weekend, we would visit Aunty Hau and her family at Barbers

Point or they would come to our house in Waipahu. Having her siblings near made all the difference in helping her cope with her loneliness.

Chapter 2:

The Foundation Mommy Laid

The example my mother set raising four children—teen-agers at that—by herself was probably what gave me the strength to realize I could raise my oldest on my own. I know we didn't make things easy for her. When she would say "no" we'd call up our dad who would usually say "yes". Aside from the guilt I'm sure he felt for not being around, I imagine he thought it was his best option for staying on our good sides.

Mommy worked in Waikiki as an accountant for a florist at the Royal Hawaiian Hotel Monday through Friday. She left home at 7:00am and returned at 6:00pm. This was her one and only job while we lived in Oahu and God was good to her. While she worked, we pretty much had the run of ourselves once we got home from school because my uncle and his family had moved back to Waimea by this time. Sometimes the neighbors would call her at work to tell her we were fighting; or we'd call her to give her our side of the story. Either way, she would pull up at 6:00pm, open the trunk of her car and pull out the black rubber hose. By then we had made up with each other and tried to convince her we were sorry. Sometimes it worked; sometimes it didn't.

At twelve years old, I was responsible for cooking dinner. Mommy would leave the shopping list on the table with the money. When I got home from school, I would walk to the store, buy the groceries, and call her when I got back home so she could tell me how to cook it. By the time she got home from work, the dinner table was set and dinner was cooked. We all sat down as a family eating, laughing, and sometimes grumbling but always enjoying each other's company. Sitting at the dinner table had always been a mandatory thing and I continued this when I had my own children. So many wonderful dinnertime memories with Mommy.

Since Mommy worked so much, the household duties of cleaning and laundry were shared by me and Lana. My brother Bronson was responsible for cleaning the yard. Randy was too little to pick up chores.

My father's career continued to prosper on Oahu as he established a name for himself, Tom "Dynamite" Dancer. One of the perks of having a father in the broadcasting industry was his connection with music promoters. All of us kids always got the best seats at concerts; not to mention the free stuff we received from sponsors. However, as his fame began to grow, we saw less and less of him.

Mommy was all we had and we were all she had. On the weekends, she took us to the Royal Sunset Drive Inn to watch the latest Bruce Lee movie. She would lay out the blanket in front of her red convertible and we'd have rice balls, fried spam, hamburger patties and pork-n-beans; it was a delicious dinner. Other times, we'd spend the day at Yokohama Beach in Makaha or the Nanakuli Tracks.

Mommy depended a lot on me and I depended a lot on her approval of the things I did. I did well in school and started working when I turned sixteen to help her out. I tried to be the perfect child in every way I could but even the perfect child messes up.

Looking back, how Mommy survived our teenage years was a miracle in itself. Maybe it was during those years when she developed her motto of God not giving you more than you could bear. We put her through a lot—pot smoking, drinking, lying, running away, overdosing on drugs, teenage pregnancies, arrests, fights, and slander. Not a single one of us could blame her for packing her bags and leaving from time to time. Each of us had our struggles and each of us dealt with life differently.

Mommy never remarried but for a couple of years she did have a boyfriend, Jim Morrison. They met at the Waianae Army Rest Camp. Jim made her happy. They enjoyed going to Campbell Industrial Park for drag car races or taking us all camping at Barbers Point. After two years of dating, Jim received notice; he was being transferred to the mainland. I overheard them arguing about his transfer. He wanted Mommy to move with him insisting she leave us with our father. He told her we didn't care for her because of the way we treated her. We did not respect her or obey her. Mommy said she couldn't leave us; we were her kids. Jim left and they remained friends throughout the years. When he got married, he introduced his new wife to Mommy over the phone. Mommy was always such an easy person to get along with.

Mommy's Hawaiian ethnicity allowed her to registered with the Department of Hawaiian Home Lands and put her name on a wait list for land and a home. In 1978, after eighteen years of waiting, she was awarded the property in Waimea on the Big Island. She was overjoyed to be moving near Kawaihae where she had grown up and would now be near her family. She left Waipahu with Randy and Lana. Bronson and I stayed at the house in Waipahu. By this time, he had a job and a family while I was in my senior year of high school with only a few months left to finish. Mommy returned for my graduation, packed up the house, and we moved everything to the Big Island.

Mommy got a job at Hawaii Preparatory Academy as an accountant and worked there for ten years. She brought home numerous exchange students from all around the world. We made them feel right at home. After she left HPA she got a position as the front desk clerk at Mauna Kea Beach Hotel; she loved this job and the people she worked with. Eventually we were all back on the Big Island, including Bronson, and each one of us found ourselves back at Mommy's house, this time with our children. Bronson had three children—Dane, Dayna and Dwight, Lana had two kids—Bradford and Brandi, and I had Kaleo.

Mommy loved having her grandchild in the house. This was the big family atmosphere she had been raised in. She was always looking out for and taking care of everybody else which is why it came as no surprise when she began struggling with her weight over the next fifteen years. Then in 1997, she was hospitalized with congested heart failure. Mommy was close to three hundred pounds; the heaviest she had ever been in her life. I believe that hospital stay really scared her because afterwards she started to care more for herself. I was so proud of the changes she was making to better her own life. She started eating healthier and enjoyed exercising. She would even walk to the grocery store instead of driving. She lost over a hundred pounds but even better than that we could tell she was happy with her new body and spirit.

When I look back on all the emotional pain Mommy had endured, from my father, myself and my siblings; I thank the Lord she put her trust in Him. I now understand, after all the pain I have been through in my own life, that trusting in God was the only way she was able to remain sane all those years. I always saw her as very independent, not realizing until later in life that she was dependent on the Lord.

Billy Graham, Oral Roberts, or some religious program was always on the TV. She loved gospel music and often sung along. Was she perfect? Are any of us? She cried, got mad, and said things she didn't mean from time to time, but she never abandoned her walk with God or her love for him. I will never know why Mommy didn't attend a church regularly; she loved the Lord and always encouraged us to trust him but preferred to have bible studies at home. Her love for the Lord kept her faithful to him and his promises are what she stood on. Her unconditional love for her children and her family along with her forgiveness are the qualities I admired most in my mom. I can only hope to live out her legacy of love and forgiveness and pass it on to my children.

Rosalie Kamila Akau laid a foundation of faith whether she realized it or not. A foundation which would carry me through my deepest, darkest moments in life.

Chapter 3:

And So, It Begins

"Aloha, this is Shirley" I answered the phone. The voice on the other end introduced herself as a nurse from North Hawaii Community Hospital. "I am calling to inform you that we have Cheyne Gambill here in the emergency room."

"What for?" I asked.

"I'm sorry but I'm not a doctor and I can't give you a diagnosis, I am just calling you because your son asked me to."

Cheyne, or Kaleo as we called him, was a bit of a daredevil so hospital calls were nothing new but the nurse's vague responses were. Again, I ask her, "What is wrong with him?"

"Like I said, I'm not a doctor and I can't answer that question."

By now I had become irritated. "Is he bleeding?"

"No." she replied, "but he is in a body splint."

I now understood she was trying to tell me his condition was serious without breaking protocol. "I'll be right there."

After hanging up the phone I had an awful feeling; had he broken his back? I called my mom and started crying, "I know Kaleo has been to the hospital a lot of times but this feels different, I can't explain it."

"Shirley, you need to lift him up to the Lord and be hopeful."

Cheyne Kaleo Gambill was born on February 28, 1980. I got the name Cheyne (pronounced Shane) out of a surf magazine. I liked the way it was spelt but unfortunately for my son, no one had ever pronounced it correctly. Since I was nineteen and unmarried when I got pregnant with him, he is my only child that carries my maiden name. I've always addressed him by his Hawaiian name, Kaleo, unless he was in trouble—that brought on the full name.

When Kaleo was two, I left his father who I had been with since the 11th grade. I broke his heart when I left and took his son. We had our differences and it seemed it was time for me to move in a different direction. Kaleo had just turned eight when I first met Lamar De Rego. Three months later, Kaleo was on his way to becoming a big brother. Marrying Lamar brought a mixture of yours, mine and ours. I brought Kaleo and he had three daughters. Then we had Auwae. Two years later Alexander was born and two years after that Duke. Lamar's daughters lived with their mom on Oahu, the two older girls didn't have an interest in getting to know their new step-mother which I understood. My father had remarried four times after my mom and I never had a relationship with any of his wives. Kaleo fully embraced his role as big brother.

Although raising four boys can have many challenges, the first of the major trials in my life did not occur until Kaleo was twenty-five years old. I wouldn't say my life was perfect before this time just somewhat uneventful. Up to that point, it seemed I had faced the average trials one might face but everything was about to change. It was a beautiful Sunday morning, March 6, 2005 to be exact. There are some dates which forever stick in your memory whether you want them to or not.

Auwae was away at boarding school, Lamar had left early in the morning with Alex and Duke to attend a cock fight in Honokaa, and Kaleo was on the phone making plans to go 4-wheeling with his friends in the mountains. As I put the finishing touches on my hair, I began to wish Kaleo was going to church with me. He had not shown much interest in church and since he was an adult, I expected that wouldn't change. But still I hoped.

The thought of bribing him to accompany me crossed my mind and I quickly dismissed it. I wanted him to attend church because he loved God not because I paid him. "Kaleo, would you like to go to church with me?"

"No thanks." He replied, "I already have plans."

I thought again about the bribe and wondered if God really would mind but decided to head to church alone. Church, as usual, was great. Our Kahu (pastor) Billy Mitchell was always very inspiring and there were a lot of times I swear he was speaking directly to me. Even times I could remember holding back tears as I thought, "How did he know that was going on in my life?"

It's amazing how God knows just what, and when, you need to hear something.

This Sunday, I cut out of the service a little early to avoid the "hello" and "goodbye" chitchat. Normally, I didn't schedule appointments on Sundays but I had a noon appointment at my office and didn't want to be late. My clients would be leaving for California later in the afternoon which meant this was the only day we could meet to get their signatures on their loan application before their trip. They arrived to the office on time and we hurried through the paperwork. During our meeting, we discovered that we both had sons named Kaleo. They had a plane to catch though so we wrapped things up, I gave them my aloha and we parted ways.

As I got into my van, my cell phone rang. Since it was an unknown number, I contemplated for a moment on whether or not I should answer it. I really didn't want to get stuck on a business call. I decided to answer the phone call and it turned out to be a nurse from North Hawaii Community Hospital informing me Kaleo had been in an accident.

After hanging up the phone I had an awful feeling; Kaleo had been to the hospital many times with minor injuries attributed to his daredevil nature but this felt much worse. I called my mom and started to cry, "I know Kaleo has been to the hospital a lot of times but this feels different, I can't explain it."

"Shirley, you need to lift him up to the Lord and be hopeful."

I knew my mom was right but I couldn't get rid of the awful feeling in my gut. As I drove to the hospital, I called Lamar and get his voicemail. No surprise since reception in Honokaa was terrible; so, I left him a message, "I'm on my way to the hospital. Kaleo's been in an accident, call me as soon as you get this message."

I started my van and headed to the hospital. On the way, I listened to a Joyce Meyer sermon on cassette tape. I often listened to this sermon while driving but today her words hit a little harder. "When hardship comes just think of it as another opportunity for God to work in your life."

I held onto her words and believed everything would be just fine. I called Lamar's phone again and left another voicemail. The next call was to my friend Sandy Shore; she agreed to meet me at the ER.

As I pulled into the parking lot at North Hawaii Community Hospital, Sandy was already there. We walk into the ER together and met my brother Randy. I assumed my mom probably told him what had happened. I looked around the waiting room wondering where Kaleo's friends were.

"I'll go check on Kaleo." Randy volunteered; he could probably tell I was afraid.

As I took a seat, I noticed Mahealani Hauanio, Kaleo's girlfriend, walking into the hospital. I had prayed the Lord would put a wonderful girl in my son's life and here she was; a beautiful Hawaiian girl, born and raised in Kalapana. They both loved the ocean, enjoyed surfing, and had many things in common. I wondered who had called her and felt bad for her to be here under such circumstances. Her carefree attitude gave me a sense of comfort. I took a deep breath and thought maybe I was overreacting. I stood up to greet her and give her a hug. "I don't have any details. Randy is checking on Kaleo right now."

A nurse passing by us stopped, "Are you Kaleo's mom?"

"Yes." I replied.

She let out a deep sigh, "He is one lucky boy."

"He is?" I felt a brief moment of relief before a thought hit me like a ton of bricks, "Could he be paralyzed?"

"Oh yes," The nurse replied, "but he is one lucky boy."

As the nurse walked away, I thought about calling our pastor. I wasn't sure how to handle the idea of my son being paralyzed but I didn't want to bother him. Mahealani and I sat down. When Randy and Sandy returned from seeing Kaleo, Sandy sat down next to me, "I think you should call Kahu Billy and have him come pray over Kaleo."

"I can make the call." Randy offered and stepped away.

Mahealani went back to see Kaleo just as his friends arrived at the hospital. They told me Kaleo had crashed his ATV while making practice runs on a field in a remote spot at the base of

Mauna Kea Mountain. One of the boys called 911 and Kaleo was airlifted from the field by the Fire Department's Rescue Helicopter, as it was too hard for an ambulance to get to the location. They brought him straight to North Hawaii Community Hospital.

Waiting to see Kaleo felt like an eternity. My mind began to think through the many times we had been in a hospital together. He had always been a thrill seeker; full of adventure without any fear. Although he had always been a great son and brother, there were many times he had gotten in trouble at school. He had been in many fights but had also experienced moments of being in the wrong place at the wrong time. Since he was the oldest, I wasn't easy on him. I embarrassed him a lot of times with my yelling and strong personality. I wish I knew then what I know now about the power of words. They can hurt even after you say sorry because saying sorry doesn't remove the deep pain hurtful words leave. I thought about how much I loved my son and how I would give anything to trade places with him if I could. Yet, here I was, sitting in a waiting room knowing I had to trust that God had a plan for him.

Mahealani came back to the waiting room and sat down. "He is fine."

I stood up feeling a sense of peace. The nurse behind the glass window saw me walking towards the door, a buzzer unlocked the doors, and she motioned for me to come walk in. "He is in room two."

I walked into the room. Kaleo was lying on a body splint with his head in a neck brace. "Hi, Kaleo." I said and gave him a kiss.

"I'm sorry, Mom." he said.

"Don't be sorry," I told him, "The nurse told me you're one lucky boy."

Another nurse was standing near the door watching us.

"If I'm so lucky," he replied, "why can't I move?" Kaleo lifted his right arm to his chest with his left hand but was unable to move it off his chest. "I can't feel the right side of my body."

I looked up to the nurse. She lowered her head and walked away from the room. The thought of Kaleo being paralyzed was too big for me. We needed God on the scene immediately. I laid my hands on Kaleo's head and began praying for the Lord to heal and comfort him.

As I finished my prayer, the doctor walked into the room and informed me of the results from Kaleo's CAT scan. "Your son has broken the fourth and fifth vertebrae in his neck. We can't be sure of how much injury has been done to the spinal cord but we need him to be very still or he could risk the chance of full body paralysis. He will be air lifted to Queens Medical Center on Oahu. They are equipped to handle injuries of this nature. We are still processing the paperwork and haven't been given a departure time yet but I will let you know as soon as I can."

With all of this information, it is now clear why the nurse had said Kaleo was a lucky boy. He was lucky to be alive and lucky he was only paralyzed on the right side rather than from the neck down. I felt an overwhelming sense of despair as I tried Lamar's cell phone again; still no answer. My brother, Randy, walked into the room with Kahu Billy Mitchell and one of the elders from the church, Zanga Schutte.

"Thank you for coming, Kahu Billy." I greeted him.

Kahu Billy said he was glad to be there for us and walked up to Kaleo. He assured him that with God all things were possible. As I stood across the bed, facing Kahu Billy, I looked into his eyes and saw how afraid he was for Kaleo. Despite the fear, we all believed God was in control. Kahu Billy anointed Kaleo's head with oil and opened his Bible to the book of Psalms chapter 91.

As he read the chapter, I began to feel touched and embraced by God's word.

"Because he loves me," says the Lord, "I will rescue him; "I will protect him, for he acknowledges my name. He will call upon me and I will answer him; I will be with him in trouble, I will deliver him and honor him." (Psalm 91:14-15 NIV)

When Kahu Billy finished reading we all laid hands on Kaleo as he prayed for him. I walked them to the waiting room and thanked both of them again for coming. Zanga assured me they were praying and believing for a victory. I held that thought as I kissed them both goodbye and promised to call them every day with updates. By this time, the waiting room had filled with family and friends. My Aunty Aggie had arrived along with my sister Lana and her daughter Brandi. My cousins Alika and Keola arrived and told me their sister, Louette, was on her way. Kyleigh Sanchez and his mom Bonnie were in the waiting room along with many of Kaleo's friends who had shown up to see if they could do anything. I noticed Mahealani was starting to feel uneasy with all the family and friends in the waiting room and wondered if she was beginning to realize Kaleo's situation was much more serious than she had imagined. I walked over and filled her in on the news I had received from the doctor. The look on her face told me Kaleo had tried to hide the seriousness from her as he assured her he was alright when he really wasn't.

When I returned to be with Kaleo, he began complaining of severe pain in his neck the nurse increases his pain medicine.

"Shirley," I looked up to see Aunty Alma Dela Santos. She was in the next room with her husband and couldn't help but over-hear everything going on. "Do you mind if I pray over your son?"

"Not at all, Aunty." I replied, welcoming any prayers I could get.

As she prayed, Kaleo was lying there with his eyes closed. I couldn't help but wonder if Kaleo even believed God could fix his situation. Around four hours later, Lamar arrived at the hospital with Alexander and Duke. I could see by his facial expression as he looked at Kaleo, he too could see this was different from all the other times Kaleo had been in the ER; this was serious. I left him with Kaleo and went to Al and Duke, in the waiting room, who were anxious to see their brother. I tried to explain to them what happened to Kaleo and told them he would be alright. Al was scared for his brother and wanted to see for himself that what I was saying was true.

When Al got back to see Kaleo lying there on the body splint board with his neck in a splint, he went to his side, folded his arms in front of him, and immediately started to cry.

"Stop crying, Al," Kaleo told him, "I'm going to be alright."

Even in all the pain he was experiencing, here he was being the strong older brother the boys have always counted on. I could see the hurt and confusion on Al's face. Kaleo was thirteen years older than him. He looked up to his brother and admired everything about him. Any sign of weakness was just not who Kaleo was in Al's eyes. Despite being very strong willed and funny, Alex was my most sensitive child and I could tell his brother's current state was scaring him.

"Alex, give your brother a kiss so Duke can come and see him too" I said.

Al gave Kaleo a kiss and a hug and we walked to the waiting room to get Duke. "If God doesn't heal him," Al looked at me, "I'll never believe in him again."

"Al," I wrapped my arm around Al's shoulder, "it's not God's fault this happened to your brother; it was an accident. We need to pray to the Lord now so he can heal your brother."

Al looked at me but didn't reply. Even though he didn't reply, I knew as he took a seat next to Randy, he would be praying for his brother like he'd never prayed before.

"Come on, Dukey." I walked with Duke to Kaleo's room. Duke and Kaleo had a special bond. He was always gentler with Duke than with Auwae and Al. Kaleo was fifteen when Duke was born and heading down a very destructive path. For this reason, I made him Duke's godfather. I had hoped it would give him a sense of responsibility.

"Hey, Buddy," Kaleo smiled as he walked into the room, "don't start crying. I'm going to be just fine. We'll go riding again when I get out of here."

Duke nodded in agreement, trying to be strong, but couldn't stop his tears.

Around 6:00pm, the doctor informed me Kaleo would probably leave North Hawaii Community Hospital around 11:00pm. There were two other people needing air transport and since Kaleo was stable, he would have to wait. I decided it would be best for me to get a flight so I could meet Kaleo at the hospital in Oahu when he landed. I booked seats for Mahealani and me to fly out at 9:30pm. Mahealani called her mom, who lived on Oahu, told her what was happening and asked if she could pick us up.

We went in together and told Kaleo of our plans.

Chapter 4:

The Strength of Family

*L*eaving Kaleo was difficult. I didn't want anything to happen to him as I was heading to the airport but I also couldn't imagine him landing at the hospital in Oahu all alone. My family and friends assured me they would stay with Kaleo until he was transported. My cousin Louette stayed by Kaleo's side from the moment I left. Louette and I had always been close and knowing she'd be with him when I left meant so much to me. This was one of the reasons I wanted to have a big family because I had always seen my family come together in times of need, even if we hadn't spent a lot of time together. God blessed us with such a great family.

Al and Duke wanted to come with me so bad but I explained they needed to stay at the house with their dad. Al was not happy and retreated to his room while Duke cried because he would miss me. As we drove to the airport, I began thinking about staying on Oahu. I had no idea how long I would need to be there but that didn't matter to me. Taking care of Kaleo was all I could think about.

We're not always able to see all the tiny pieces God is working together for our good when everything is in motion. Now that some time has passed, I am able to see how amazing it was for me to afford spur of the moment airfare not only for me but for Mahealani too. The fact that a flight was even available to take us to Oahu on such short notice was another blessing from God. I know God was working for Kaleo and for me.

We arrived on Oahu at 10:30pm and Kathy Castillo, Mahealani's mom, picked us up from the airport. When I called North Hawaii Hospital to see if Kaleo had been transported from the hospital to the airport, I found out his time had been moved to 1:30am due to a pilot shift change. Air ambulance pilots were only allowed to fly so many flights in a 24-hour period and the pilot on duty needed to be replaced.

Mahealani and I spent the night with her mother and step-father in Ewa Beach. We planned to leave for Queens Medical Center first thing in the morning but falling asleep seemed almost impossible. Exhaustion finally took over around 1:00am but I soon awoke from the sound of Kathy's husband returning from work. He was a police officer and had been working the graveyard shift. As I was lying in bed, awake once again, I felt such sorrow for Kaleo. Kathy had many pictures of him and Mahealani around the house and seeing them together made everything feel surreal. How could we be going through this horrible mess? I hid my face in the pillow and cried my heart out. "God, let Kaleo arrive safely at the hospital."

I called my cousin Louette at 5:30am. "What time did Kaleo finally leave?"

"He's still here, Sis." Louette replied, "The air ambulance had to pick up a boy in Hilo first but Kaleo is scheduled to leave next; sometime around 11:00am."

"It's been over fifteen hours."

"I know, I know." Louette replied in a soothing voice, "Kaleo is doing good, he will be there soon, Sis."

Mahealani walked into the room. "I heard you on the phone."

I filled her in on what was happening and broke down in tears. I couldn't believe Kaleo was still on Waimea. I felt so sorry for him. After we decided to get up and get ourselves ready, I decided to call Kaleo's father, David. Even though it had been fifteen years since we spoke, I still had his parent's home phone number memorized. His sister, Christine, answered the phone and I explained to her what had happened with Kaleo. She told me David lived on Kaua'i now but she was going to let him know what was going on.

Kathy made us breakfast and, while we were eating, Darryl walked into the kitchen. This was the first time I had met him. He said a quick hello and then told us he was going to leave us girls to our breakfast before retreating to yard work. I thought it was strange for him to have worked all night and then wake up to do yard work. Later Darryl would share with me that this incident involving Kaleo had brought back memories of his oldest daughter who had died as an infant and he just didn't know what to say to me.

Mahealani and I arrived to the hospital around the same time Kaleo's ambulance arrived. The doctors had to do their examination and go over the medical records from North Hawaii Community Hospital so I had to spend a little time in the waiting room. My cousin, Danny Akau, arrived at the hospital; a sight for sore eyes. We hadn't seen each other in over nine years. We kissed and hugged each other wishing our reunion had been under better circumstances.

Then, in walked my thirteen-year-old son, Auwae. He had been attending Kamehameha School, a private school on Oahu, for the past year. His dorm advisor Mr. Nakanishi told Auwae about Kaleo's accident and brought him to the hospital to meet me. I was so happy to see him although his face was covered in concern. I tried to ease his worries and tell him everything would be alright. Kaleo was in the best hospital, getting the best care. Mr. Nakanishi brought a box of manapua and offered it to everyone. With our group in the waiting room growing, I decided to find out if Kaleo was settled in. The nurse asked me who I was there to see and after telling her Kaleo's story she directed me to his room.

*Manapua:
a Chinese bun with
meat; it's a popular
dish in Hawaii.*

Queens Medical Center was nothing like our little ER at North Hawaii Community Center; it was really busy with lots of doctors and nurses moving and tending to patients. Kaleo was at the end of the corridor in the last room. When I pull the curtains and walked into his room, to my astonishment, I found my son in severe pain. A male nurse was standing over him with a clip board in hand asking him what was wrong. I couldn't believe my eyes!

Kaleo was crying and trying to lift his body up moving around as much as he could. I rushed over to his side. "Kaleo, remember what the doctor said? You need to stay still or you could risk severing your spinal cord."

"It hurts too bad, mom." Kaleo cried.

I looked at the male nurse. "Can't you give him something for the pain?"

The nurse informed me that he needed to finish asking all the questions because it was part of the hospital procedure.

"Everything you need to know should be in the paperwork which was transported with my son."

He shook his head. "I don't have anything."

"Mom," Kaleo looked at me, "I'm trying to be respectful but it hurts."

I was also trying to be respectful but having had enough of the nonsense I proceeded to the middle of the ER corridor and at the top of my voice shouted, "I know Queen's Medical Center is the best trauma unit in the Pacific Basin but my son has just been airlifted here from the Big Island with a broken neck. He is in severe pain and should not be moving because he can severe his spinal cord and there is a nurse in his room asking him questions."

I now had the attention of everyone. Doctors and nurses came running to Kaleo's room. My cousin Danny rushed to Kaleo's side trying to comfort him as he cried because of the pain. A female doctor rushed to Kaleo's side and started an IV with morphine to calm him down. They transported him off the gurney unto a hospital bed and got him ready to be taken to the critical care unit on the fourth floor. Danny escorted Kaleo along with the nurses to his room as I gathered everyone from the ER waiting room.

My mom always taught me to be respectful to others.; a lesson I passed along to my children. But like a lioness protecting her cubs sometimes you have to ROAR.

After Kaleo was settled into his room, the nurses began doing their best to get him comfortable. By this time, it had been twenty-four hours since the accident and he was asking for food. Unfortunately, they told him he'd have to wait until after he saw the doctor.

Family and friends continued to arrive and bring well wishes, support and food.

The hospital social worker informed me that because Kaleo's recovery could take some time, I should consider the apartment complex attached to the hospital. There was a room available but she wanted to know if I had any problems climbing stairs because it was located on the third floor. The cost was fifty dollars a night. I considered this a blessing since I could stay at the hospital near Kaleo. Auwae ended up staying with me at the apartment as well since he found it too difficult to go back to school and concentrate.

We all sat and talked with each other in the waiting room, my mom's youngest sister Aunty Haunani and her daughter Stephenie arrived with so much food it looked like we had our own buffet. When you don't know what to say or do, food is always the best way to show your love. I hadn't seen my Aunty in years and it feels so good to see her and hug her. She took care of me when I was growing up, and I was Stephenie's babysitter. I hadn't realized how much I had missed them.

The hospital staff was very nice to our growing support group. I think they realized how serious Kaleo's condition was and had compassion for us. As long as we were not loud or getting out of hand, no one seemed to bother us.

Finally, Dr. Misunaga arrived in the waiting room. Danny and I stepped outside in the courtyard with the doctor. "Kaleo has broken the fourth and fifth vertebrae in his neck. We are not sure how much damage has been done to the spinal cord but he needs an operation to fix the break. During the operation there is a possibility that he could experience seizures or a stroke. If this happens there is not much we can do because we'll be focused on infusing the break in his neck. We'll put a halo on him that will be screwed into his forehead to keep the neck from moving." He went on to tell us that the operation would take at least five hours.

I couldn't believe everything I was hearing. "On a scale of one to ten, with ten being the worst, what are we looking at here?"

He stared at me with deep compassion and replied, "Nine."

I broke down and started crying. My cousin Danny was crying as well and I could see through the window the rest of the family could tell the news was bad. After Dr. Misunaga left, Danny assured me that Kaleo was in God's hands and he would be all right. When we walked back into the waiting room, I look around for Mahealani. I could tell by the look on her face she now realized just how serious Kaleo's injuries were. I sat down by her and comforted her. "Kaleo is in God's hands. We're going to trust God for his healing."

Kaleo and Mahea had been dating for almost two years. I knew she was a strong-willed person and wanted to believe what I said was true; but I could tell she was scared. She walked outside into the courtyard to process everything I just told her. I was worried about her and hoped her mom would return soon to help comfort her. My Aunty Haunani sat down by me, "Are you okay?"

I nodded. I couldn't say much because I was still trying to process everything Dr. Misunaga had just told me. Through the window, I noticed Mahea was now curled up in the corner of the window seal sobbing. I walked out to her and hugged her.

"I called my aunt and she is praying for Kaleo too." she told me.

After letting her cry for a bit, I brought her back into the waiting room.

"Can we see Kaleo?" she asked.

I nodded and we walked back to his room together. When Kaleo saw Mahea, his face immediately lit up. He smiled really big as if to tell her everything was okay. She decided to stay with Kaleo in the room so I helped her settle in and checked with the nurses that it was okay before leaving them. His surgery was scheduled for the next day and visiting hours are almost over. When I asked why they were waiting so long, I was told they needed to wait for the swelling to go down before operating.

I kissed Kaleo. "I'll see you in the morning son."

"Thanks for everything, Mom." he replied, "See you tomorrow."

I held back my tears as I headed towards the waiting room. Family and friends said their goodbyes so Auwae and I could head to our room and get some rest. I had no appetite but out of concern for Auwae I stopped at a vending machine to grab him a sandwich and drink. Although our room was comfortable, I had so much on my mind. All I wanted to do was find a place to sit and cry. I had held it together, for the most part, all day and I was exhausted. But I continued to hold it together for Auwae. I didn't want him to worry.

Alex called me, concerned for Kaleo. I updated him on everything I could then told him to continue praying for his brother. "God answers prayers and he will heal Kaleo. We need to believe this."

"Yes, Mom." he replied, "I love you."

"I love you too, Al."

Duke wanted to talk to me next. I assured him Kaleo was in good hands and told him he too needed to pray for his brother before he went to bed.

"I will Mom, I love you,"

"I love you too, Duke."

The boys said Lamar had already gone to bed. I was disappointed that he hadn't called once since I left last night. The boys were so worried for their brother. At least I knew my family would stop by to check on the boys for me. I called my mom to fill her in on the events of the day.

"Shirley, the Lord won't let you suffer more than you can bear. He loves you very much. Kaleo is in Jehovah's hand; trust in him."

I think back now on the advice my mother gave me that night and how much peace it brought me. Especially since it came from her. She was such a rock. No matter how shaky things got in life, we all knew we could find Mommy as the one constant who would not waiver.

Auwae was busy trying to work on homework while I made calls but it was now almost 10:00pm. I knew we were both exhausted and suggested it was time to go to sleep.

Chapter 5:

The Miracle I Needed

he deep chop, chop, chop of a helicopter flying by ripped me from my sleep. If I wasn't in a room, I could have sworn it was landing next to our bed. As I laid in bed, I began doubting God's ability to heal Kaleo. Three o' clock in the morning and lack of sleep didn't make a very good combination for positive thinking. I contemplated the quality-of-life Kaleo could face. He had always been very athletic as a child; he played pop warner football, little league baseball, and basketball for parks and recreation. During high school, he played basketball and football, then later took up boxing. He loved the ocean, surfing, diving, fishing, hunting, and now had a new found passion for racing ATV's and dirt bikes. How would all that change if things did not go well during his surgery?

There had never been a dull moment with him and I couldn't imagine him any other way. The best quality he possessed was the love he had for his little brothers. Where most older brothers don't have time for their younger brothers, he enjoyed having them around. He taught them so many things and they were better men because of his lessons.

Lamar was strict with the boys, they were not allowed to have any tattoos, earrings, different colored hair or fancy haircuts before the age of eighteen. Once they became adults, they pretty much could do what they wanted to their bodies. Kaleo had a lot of respect for Lamar and a little fear too I'd say, so he waited until he was eighteen before going wild in these areas. He tattooed GAMBILL across his back, put an earring in each ear lobe and dyed his hair blonde! He was respectful but certainly his own person.

How could this be happening to him?

I got out of bed, sat in the small living room, and started to read my bible and pray to the Lord for help. The thought of God not being able to heal him crossed my mind and I prayed if that was the case, he would just take him. I wasn't sure Kaleo would survive with any kind of limited mobility. That wouldn't go along with his no fear nature at all. Then I thought of Mahealani, it wouldn't be fair to ask her to take care of Kaleo. What was I thinking? I had to stop thinking these thoughts. I began crying and tried to muffle my cry so I wouldn't wake Auwae.

"Mom, are you alright?"

Apparently, I wasn't very good at being quiet. "I'm fine, Auwae, go back to sleep." I looked at my watch it was 4:00am. I took a breath as I tried to think about who might be awake for me to talk to. I knew my brother Randy would be leaving for work so I decided I would call him. "I need to step outside and get some air. I'll be back."

I walked downstairs and saw that someone was already in the pool. I didn't want them to hear my phone conversation so I walked to the sidewalk outside the apartment building.

"Hello?" Randy's sleepy voice indicated I must have woken him.

"Ran, It's me."

"How's, Kaleo?"

"Not good." I broke down crying as I told him everything the doctor said and all the things that could possibly go wrong during the surgery. "I just wish I could trade places with him. I've lived a good life. Kaleo is still so young. He has his whole life ahead of him, he doesn't need all of this."

Randy started crying and I heard someone in the background asking what was going on. As Randy began updating the person, I realized it was my brother. "Bronson said to tell you that God is the great physician and he can do all things. Hang in there, Shirley. We will find the next flight out and meet you at the hospital."

"I'll see you soon." I hung up the phone and couldn't help but appreciate how God worked in mysterious ways. Bronson and I had a falling out some time ago. He and I did that a lot in our lives, hold grudges against each other for some reason or another. Pride will get you all the time! Now here he was on his way to Oahu to support me. Knowing my brothers would soon be at the hospital was comforting.

Honolulu was waking up, the sidewalk was getting busy, people were moving about, cars were on the streets; it was going to be a long day. I knew Auwae must be wondering where I was so I went back to the room. It was only 6:30am but I was anxious to see what kind of night Kaleo had and how Mahealani was doing so Auwae and I headed to the hospital.

Mahealani told me Kaleo had a rough night because he was so hungry. The accident happened on Sunday and it was now Tuesday. He was begging for food but because of the surgery he was only allowed water and ice chips. He was beginning to get a little angry so the nurses sedated him to help ease the tension. Mehealani headed back to our room to freshen up and get some rest while me and Auwae went for breakfast; but I didn't dare tell Kaleo that.

My mom called to give me words of encouragement and let me know she was thinking of me. I knew Alexander and Duke were already on their way to school so I would have to check in with them when they got home. Kahu Billy called to check in and I gave him an update as well. He told me the church was praying for Kaleo's healing and if I needed anything they would be there for me and my family. While I was sitting in the waiting room with Auwae, making all my update phone calls, the elevator doors opened and out stepped my cousin Danny along with my brothers, Bronson and Randy. Seeing them gave me a sense of comfort; something inside of me just knew everything would be alright. From that moment on I believed total healing for Kaleo. I hugged both my brothers and started to cry.

I told Bronson how sorry I was for what was going on between us and I asked for his forgiveness. I felt really safe to have my brothers and my cousin with me. They immediately went in to see Kaleo. Seeing him here at Queens Medical Center was a lot different than seeing him at North Hawaii Community Hospital. I believe the reality of how intense his injury was combined with seeing him is what brought them to tears. Throughout the day, the waiting room began to fill with family and friends once again. Everyone was there to support us and pray for Kaleo. The love was so overwhelming.

Aunty Haunani, and my cousin Stephenie had both took the day off of work to be with me. Aunty Haunani had always been that way. Anytime family was in town for whatever reason she always tried to help out. And help out she did, the boxes of Chinese food she brought with her for breakfast were amazing.

Kaleo's dad David arrived with his mom and his sisters, Christine and Eleanor, along with some of Kaleo's cousins. Although David had arrived the day before while Kaleo was in the ER, we hadn't yet had a chance to talk yet. We sat down to talk and it felt as if it had just been yesterday when we last saw each other. We laughed and talked about old times in Waipahu. I was glad to hear he and his wife, Melinda, were doing well in Kauai. He had a strong faith and also believed the Lord could heal Kaleo.

God's peace and love is amazing. When I left David, there were many bad feelings between us and his family too. They weren't happy with me taking Kaleo away. But here in this moment, God was at the center of each of our lives and it was impossible not to change. Impossible not to forgive. The bad feelings between us were gone. We had come together for Kaleo. Although many years had passed, we still had the same respect and love for one another that we had before I had left him.

Everyone took turns sitting with Kaleo in ICU. He didn't make it easy for anyone in the room because he would not stop begging for food. All we could do was wait and wait some more. As I look around the waiting room filled with family and friends, I began to wish Lamar was with us.

Despite all we were facing, looking around the waiting room helped me realize we were not the only ones facing difficult times. Other families were gathered around to support their loved ones as well. One particular family stood out to me because they were also waiting to hear results for their son who had contacted leptospirosis while working on the side of the roadway in dirty water puddles. His mother informed me she was very worried. The doctors had told her family they would be taking her son to surgery in a few minutes. The infection was so bad that in order to save her son's life they would be amputating both of his legs below the knees and both of his arms below the elbows. Her and her husband were trying to be strong but they were full of uncertainty for what the future would hold. I recognized this because I found myself feeling the same in regards to Kaleo.

"I'll be praying for your son." I told her as the doctor called her name for an update before the surgery.

"Thank you."

As she and her husband walked up to the doctor, I prayed God's peace and comfort be with their whole family then went back to waiting to hear about my own son. Around 5:00PM, Dr. Misunaga arrived to tell me Kaleo's surgery was scheduled for 8:00PM and would be approximately five hours. Knowing the surgery had finally been scheduled brought little relief because we were still uncertain what the outcome would be. I went to visit Kaleo and let him know the surgery had finally been scheduled.

The ICU Nurse let us gather in Kaleo's room to pray over him before they took him for surgery. Myself, Auwae, my brothers, Kaleo's dad David and his sisters all laid our hands on him as I began to pray, I could tell Kaleo was getting agitated with me as I was insisting he pray for himself too. His Aunty Eleanor said it was alright if he didn't but I insisted he repeat after me. I needed him to believe God could heal him. Just like Kahu Billy did at North Hawaii Community Hospital, I recited Psalm 91 over Kaleo. Only this time it came alive to me.

"Because he loves me," says the Lord, "I will rescue him; I will protect him, for he acknowledges my name. He will call upon me, and I will answer him; I will be with him in trouble, I will deliver him and honor him. With long life will I show him my salvation." (Psalm 91:14-16 NIV)

I needed Kaleo to acknowledge the Lord. David, my brother Bronson and I escorted Kaleo all the way to the OR with lifted hands praising God for his healing. When the OR elevator door opened, the male nurse on the other side was shocked to see us in the elevator with Kaleo. As the elevator doors closed, my brother shouted, "We're praying for you, Doc!"

We all gathered in the waiting room with our pillows and blankets. Since the doctor had told me the surgery would take up to five hours I wondered if something had gone wrong when he showed up in the waiting room around 11:00PM.

The doctor walked up to me, "The surgery went better than expected. Kaleo didn't need the halo. He's currently in ICU and will be moved to recovery soon."

The next day we all went to visit Kaleo. I think the staff gave him his own room so they wouldn't have to worry about us bothering any other patients. They even allowed us to use the room next to his for all the food which continued to come in.

Kaleo was twenty-five when the accident happened. He is now forty-two. Back then I was begging God to do something for my son. Even though, at the time, I considered it a miracle for Kaleo; today I honestly think the miracle we experienced was an answer to my prayers; a miracle for me. God knew I would need to see how great and mighty he was; how he was capable of the impossible. There were so many amazing things to reflect on amongst what seemed to be an awful experience at the time. I am sure I may have missed some but here are the ones I can remember:

Kaleo's father and his family visited with us while we were at the hospital. Although we had parted on bad terms, nobody spoke ill about me or mentioned me taking Kaleo away from them. We supported each other during this difficult period and came together for Kaleo.

The pastor from my church would check in with me often to find out how Kaleo was doing. I knew my church family was praying hard for our situation. They were believing God would perform a miracle on Kaleo's behalf. I thought the miracle was him coming out of the surgery.

After the surgery, doctors said only time would tell what kind of damage may have been caused. Kaleo entered rehab and it seemed that he might suffer from some paralysis. He would sit himself up in the bed but would fall over because he couldn't hold himself up. When I told the pastor how the surgery had gone and gave him the update on the paralysis, he stopped me and said, "Shirley, remember, we are praying for one hundred percent healing, nothing less."

Even though logic was against us, I believed with him and replied, "Yes, yes."

On the third day, Kaleo was transferred to Rehab Hospital of the Pacific where he went through extensive rehab. Even though rehab was difficult, Kaleo kept his humorous demeanor about him; immediately making friends. At the rehab facility, there was a boy visiting from Europe who had dove into the water and broke his neck. Kaleo became wheelchair buddies with him. Since my cousin Danny lived near, he would visit Kaleo every day and push him around in the wheelchair. Then I would go down every weekend with one of his brothers. On one of the weekends, we took him to Red Lobster because he was wanting lobster so bad. He ended up eating so much lobster and butter that he woke up in the middle of the night with his eyes swollen shut.

Even though Auwae and Duke were able to see Kaleo in the rehab facility, Alex never got a chance to visit because Kaleo was only there for eight days before he was released. Praise God! On March 20ᵗʰ 2005 Kaleo walked off the plane. My eyes had seen a miracle, my life was changed forever.

Although this could have been a life-changing event, Kaleo didn't live his life as though he was a miracle. When he and Mahea returned home, he announced he was going to marry Mahea. Or in his words, "I don't care if I have to crawl down the aisle. I am marrying her as soon as I can."

The wedding date was set for October 8, 2005.

Mommie Rosalie Kamila Akau Gambill

Mommie and Dad at my wedding Nov. 2, 1991,
My Dad was excited to walk me down the aisle.

Mommie with her kids. Me, Lana, Bronson
(top left) and Randy (I miss him)

Kaleo always pushed the limits…doing what he loved!

Kaleo with his Grandma Nana Suliven and Mahealani recovering from his
neck injury at the Rehab of the Pacific on Oahu. It's the only picture I have
of him from his accident. I never wanted any pictures taken of him
after the accident. I witnessed a miracle – his healing.

BJ Penn's 'Just Scrap" MMA Fight in Hilo…Kaleo won his fight.
Uncle Danny Akau on the left and Uncle Bronson Gambill on the right.
Two of his biggest supporters.

Kaleo Wedding Party October 8, 2005 – two weeks after we lost Alex.
He wanted to cancel the wedding, I insisted we move forward,
it's what Alex would have wanted for his brother.

Kaleo and his family.
Mahealani and their daughter Hualili'omalie aka Lily! aka My Love!

Kaleo receiving his brown belt in Jiu Jitsu – always trying to better himself.

Cheyne Kaleo Gambill – My oldest son

1993 Halloween–me and Alexander 6 months old

Alex night diving with Auwae, cousin Kapanai'a and Duke,
holding his prize lobster

Alex up to bat – West Hawaii Little League Allstar Team 2002

Alex at May Day Waimea Elementary School

Alexander Bennett Hing Wai De Rego – Al Boy–He loved his Hawaiian
Heritage. Alex was my third child and the most inquisitive of them all.
Always asking question and speaking his mind.

Kaawaloa Kona Hawaii, the ocean was anything but calm that dreadful night

Rescue Helicopter – Family and Friends looking for Alex

I am in disbelief but still hopeful we will find Alex. My Aunty Leo Akau
sitting on the rocks behind me.
Hawaii County Fire Captain trying to comfort me.

Bronson Duke Nainoa De Rego – 9th Grade picture Honoka'a High School
(2009 / 2010 school year) Duke was the baby of the bunch,
the youngest of my sons.

Duke 2009 Freshman Homecoming Escort. Great picture of Duke one of
my favorites. Lamar always making a funny face.

Homecoming Night – after the football game. Duke was so proud to
be a football player and represent his freshman class as Homecoming Escort.
I was so proud of him too; I know he worked so hard
on and off the football field.

Duke and his cousin Chris Gambill on their ATV's – we would go back
to Kaawaloa almost every weekend after losing Alex, just being in that
area made us feel closer to Alex. The boys would ride around looking
for any sign of Alex. Duke missed his brother and longed for him.

Duke loved baseball – we called him the 'homerun hitter" he had to hit
homeruns, or the coach would put in a pitch runner for him.
He cruised the bases running home!

Duke May Day King 2008 – Waimea Middle Public Conversion Charter
School I was so proud of all his hard work he put in to
receive his nomination for King.

8th grade graduation Duke and his classmate Jessica Benioni –
she was also the May Day Queen.

Auwae all checked into his dormitory at Kamehameha School
Kapalama Campus. It was so hard to leave him there.
I remember crying all the way to the airport.

Auwae University of Arizona – I looked forward to the few games
I was able to attend in person while Auwae played football at U of A.
It was a lifetime experience for sure! Auwae is my second oldest son.

The boys, Alex and Cousin Chace on top bleacher making signs with their hands. Cousin Chris, Auwae and Kien right below them, and a friend. Just one of many basketball games that were a big part of the boys growing up. My brother Randy was responsible for always keeping the boys active in sports. They had no choice because he was the coach.

Kien and I

Ululii and her husband Robert

The one thing I regret was not taking more pictures with me and the boys. Here is one of us, Kaleo, me Auwae and Duke. This was taken after one of Kaleo's MMA fights in 2009.

Chapter 6:

Gives and Takes Away

Raising boys can be quite the handful at times. Kaleo and Alexander were both very adventurous and independent, Auwae was calmer and enjoyed being close, and Duke was my little opihi. The opihi is a small shell urchin that sticks to rocks in the ocean. The minute you touch an opihi, it sucks itself to the rock and you cannot get it off. Duke was my opihi, I swear there were times you literally had to pry him off me. Four boys plus four different personalities meant I was always on my toes.

Kaleo sought out adventure and was fearless, Alex admired him and wanted to be doing whatever his big brother was doing. With Kaleo and Mahea's wedding date drawing near, Kaleo and a few friends planned a camping trip to spear fish for the wedding. I knew Al would no doubt want to join him if he ever found out but the trip was on a Friday and I did not want him to miss school. So, I decided not to tell him.

I made it to Thursday, September 22, 2005—the day before the trip—and Al had not said anything about the trip. It seemed as though I was in the clear. My desk phone rang that afternoon; Ms. Ontiveros of Waimea Intermediate School was calling to tell me Alex had not been behaving in school today.

"Thank you for your call. I'll speak with him when I get home from work." I hung up the phone. Although Alex was pretty popular in school there were some areas he was struggling in academically and I was sure that contributed to the days he misbehaved. As I was thinking about Alex, my phone rang again.

"Hi, Mom, how are you today?"

"Hi, Al," I replied, "I just got a call from your teacher."

"I know." He sighed, "I'm trying my best in school." Before I had time to reply he changed the subject, "I just witnessed Pono's dog give birth, can I have a puppy?"

"No." I shook my head and laughed. How did this kid go from trouble at school to bringing home a puppy?

"Kaleo's going camping tomorrow with Uncle David, can I go?"

There was the question I was hoping to stay away from. "No, you have school tomorrow."

"Can I go to Honokaa with Pono and watch his basketball practice?"

Surprised by the quick recovery I agreed. "Alright. I'll see you when I get home from work"

I hung up the phone and knowing the camping trip discussion was probably not over. Dinner was great and Alex seemed extra helpful, doing everything he could to clean the kitchen. Then he asked about the camping trip again. "Al, you can't go camping with Kaleo tomorrow, you have school."

His chipper, helpful demeaner faded as he stormed out of the kitchen. "Please can I go with Kaleo?" he shouted from his bed, "I promise I'll be good in school."

His promises went on for about an hour before he finally fell asleep. I laid in bed wondering what his day would be like at school. Would he be distracted from not going on the trip and get in trouble? The thought of keeping him home crossed my mind but I knew I had a busy day at the office and couldn't stay home with him. "God, help Al to have a good night sleep." I quietly prayed, "And renew his spirit."

A loud slam from the backdoor woke me from my sleep. I looked at the time, 6:00AM.

"Al, you coming?" Kaleo yelled.

"Oh no." I sighed.

Sure enough, Alex came into my room crying, "No, she's not going to let me go."

Alex dropped down on the bed crying while Kaleo stood in the doorway staring at me.

I sighed. "Okay."

Alex sat up with a huge smile on his face. "I can go?"

"Yes, but only this one time, Alex. I'm not letting you stay home from school to go anywhere else."

"I love you." he jumped off the bed and ran down the hallway, "I love you, Mom."

Kaleo smiled at me and shook his head. "Hurry up," he yelled, "we're late. Uncle David is waiting for us"

I hurried out of bed and rushed down the hallway. "Get a jacket and towels."

"Don't forget to take some food." I hollered as he returned to his bedroom, "Where's your extra clothes?"

He came out of his room with a long sleeve shirt on and a beach towel draped across his shoulders. "Mom, I'm not a baby anymore"

"We don't need food." Kaleo shouted from the door, "We'll stop at the store"

"I love you, mom." Alex said as he ran out of the house and jumped into the passenger seat of Kaleo's Ford F3500 truck. I waved to the boys as they drove off. My twenty-five-year-old and twelve-year-old off to do what they loved best—camping and fishing—outdoor adventures.

As I approached the end of my workday, I realized how much different the day might have gone if I had forced Alex to go to school. At some point, I probably would have received a call from his teacher or principal to pick him up. I got into the car and headed home to start my weekend. With only two more weeks until the wedding, Duke and I were planning to go shopping for wedding outfits for him and Alex. I was hoping to find something nice for me as well. I had promised him that if we got up early, did our house chores and finished the shopping we would go to the movies. He'd go anywhere with me, my little opihi!

I called to check on Kaleo and Al before heading to bed. They were settled in at their campsite Keopuka, a place I was not

Ulua are large fish native to the Indian Ocean and western Pacific Ocean.

familiar with and the first time Kaleo had been there as well. The locals called the area Rock in the Water. It was well-known for Ulua fishing and a popular site with the local fisherman. There was a special permit required to be on the site which was obtained months in advance. I was a bit surprised to hear that of the ten fishermen who had signed up for the trip only two others had arrived—Uncle David Herring and his son, Yuki.

Saturday morning was beautiful. Duke and I breezed through the shopping list for Party Supply and Walmart before heading to the movies. I called Kaleo's phone and asked to speak with Al. "Do you want us to come pick you up?"

"No," he replied, "I'll stay with Kaleo."

"Okay."

Al began talking about the uhu (parrot fish) fish he had caught. He was so proud of himself. It reminded me of the time he went diving for lobsters with my brother, Bronson. Even though his snorkel had been leaking, he never complained because he loved diving and fishing. He continued on about the amazing catch for a bit before sounding like he was ready to go.

"I love you, Al."

"I love you, Mom."

"Let me know if you change your mind. Duke and I will pick you up." I hung up the phone pretty confident he wouldn't be changing his mind.

I wasn't sure I would enjoy the movie because my mind was spinning with all the things left to do for the wedding. But I actually enjoyed taking a break and relaxing in the theater. After the movies, we stopped at K-mart and Costco. Although Duke had been a champ, I could tell he was as glad to be done with the shopping as I was. I called Lamar and told him we were running late and I wouldn't be home in time to cook dinner for him. I suggested he meet us at Paniolo Country Inn for dinner. We finished dinner around 8:00pm and on the way home, I swung by my mom's house to give my cousin, Mapuana, a ride home to her house since it was on the way. As I left the restaurant, I tried calling Kaleo to check in but he did not answer. When I pulled into my mom's driveway, I had a strange feeling and tried Kaleo's phone again.

"Hello?"

My cousin hopped into the car.

"Hi, Kaleo, how's everything?"

"I can't find Al, Mom."

"What?" I asked thinking maybe I heard him wrong.

"I can't find Al, Mom." He repeated.

"What do you mean you can't find Al, Kaleo?" I think about the dark secluded area they are camping in, "You better find your brother."

"I'm trying." he replied, "He went to the bathroom."

"I'm on my way home." I tell him, "I'll call you when I get there."

"Everything okay?" Mapuana asked.

I shook my head. I had a bad feeling. I dropped her off and got to the house. Lamar was sitting on the couch watching TV "Kaleo said he cannot find Al."

"Shirley, you're overreacting. It's probably just dark and he couldn't see him."

"I don't know, Lamar, I have a bad feeling about this. You call Kaleo and talk to him."

Lamar called Kaleo and soon sat up on the couch, "What do you mean you think he fell into the water? Call 911, Kaleo." I started screaming hysterically. "Shut up!" Lamar yelled, "I can't hear. Kaleo, we're on our way."

"Is Al, okay?" Duke cried next to me.

We followed Lamar to the pickup. I tried calling my brothers, Bronson and Randy, neither of them answered but I left them hysterical messages. I didn't dare call my mom until I had more information. She wasn't in the best of health, and I didn't want the stress to send her to the hospital. I grabbed hold of Lamar's hand as I quietly pray for God's favor.

"Get your seatbelt on." I yelled at Duke as Lamar sped down the road.

"He thinks Al fell into the ocean? How can that be?" I questioned Lamar.

Lamar kept his eyes on the road and never responded. I could see the fear in his eyes and could only imagine the thoughts running through his mind.

Duke was crying, "Is Al going to be, okay?"

I looked to the backseat. With Auwae away at school, Duke and Alex had gotten very close. I couldn't imagine what thoughts must be going through his mind. We were on our way back to Kona, an hour drive, and from there to the campsite it was another twenty minutes. The pickup was eerily quiet with the exception of Duke's sobs and my prayers

Just past Konawena High School, we took a side road off the main highway. I looked at the clock on the dash, we made it here in forty-five minutes. David was waiting for us and we were now following him down the dark mountainside road through bushes and trees. Lamar followed closely behind him careful not to leave the trail.

I could see the helicopter flying as they shined their light down on the water. There was an ambulance with flashing lights in the distance but it looked so far away. The road was bumpy with tall grass on either side of it. Lamar stayed close to David's truck so we wouldn't stray from the path. The tires hit something and I heard Lamar swear as we slid down the mountain. When we finally reached the campsite, I stepped out of the truck and realized we were on lava rocks. I couldn't really make out much of my surroundings because it was so dark.

"Stay in the truck." I yelled at Duke as me and Lamar made our way to the edge of what looked like a cliff. Divers were in the water with lights and Kaleo was standing on a rock telling them where to check. The ocean was so rough. The water was slamming into the rocks below us and to the right of us there was a large blow-hole spewing water out all around us every few seconds. There was rock all around me. Never have I been so terrified of the ocean as I was in that moment. Every crash of a wave felt like a hammer to my heart. I couldn't breathe.

Lamar held me. "I love you, Shirley." He held me tight, "I'm so scared."

"I'm scared too, Lamar." I managed to reply, "We just have to trust in the Lord."

A group of firemen walked over to us, the beams of their searchlights dancing across the rocks as they approached. They told us they were going to search the terrain and see if Alex had fallen somewhere on the rocks and got hurt. Lamar told me he was going to help them search for Al.

Kaleo ran up to me crying, "I'm so sorry, Mom, I'm sorry."

I held on to him and let him cry. "It's going to be alright. God wouldn't let anything happen to your brother; we have to believe that." I said wanting to comfort my son's pain but I had no idea what would happen. I felt as if I was back at the theater watching a movie with Duke, but instead of actors we were the family living out the story unfolding in front of us. I held Kaleo tight, "We need to be strong and keep looking for Alex."

Lamar returned with the firemen, no sign of Alexander. He had fallen during the search and now had a gash on his knee but didn't want the paramedics to look at it. Kaleo and Lamar were talking but mostly crying with one another.

The fire captain walked up and told us the divers needed to get out of the water because the ocean was too rough. It was now 11:00PM and they decided the search would have to resume at first light for the safety of those searching. "I don't think Alex fell in the water." The fire captain stated, "His brother said he had slippers on and we haven't found any slippers floating in the water. It was more likely that he fell somewhere on land."

Two more vehicles were making their way down the mountain. When the first truck got closer, I realized it was my cousin Louette, her husband Nelson, and their daughters, Lahele and Kehau. I ran to her crying.

"Your mom called me." She told me.

In the other truck was Louette's brothers, Alika and Keola, and they had my brother Randy with them. Randy had gotten my voice message while he and his family were in the movies. They came immediately but couldn't get down the mountain in their van so he waited for someone to come along. We all stood there crying as I told them what we had been told. Now that his cousins were there, I brought Duke out of the truck.

Louette's husband, Nelson, a retired fire fighter, began talking to the fire captain. My head was spinning from the chaos of the situation and the dark surroundings only added to the confusion.

"Auntie." Yuki, David's son, walked up to me, "I think Alex fell in the ocean."

"Why do you think that, Yuki? The fire captain said he didn't think he was in the ocean."

"The rope was broken and Kaleo had to tie it back together for us to walk across."

I walked up to Kaleo. "Kaleo, was the rope broken?"

"Yes." he replied, "But David thought he saw Al's light at the camp."

To get from one fishing area to another you needed to cross a plank and along the plank was a rope to guide your way. I told the fire captain what Yuki had said about the rope, but the water was still too rough to search. All we could do was wait until morning.

I watched in disbelief as the ambulance and fire truck drove up the mountain.

Duke and his cousins were sitting together under the make-shift tent at the campsite trying to comfort one another. The adults were sitting by the ocean watching the current. We had left the house in such a hurry I didn't grab anything and the air was starting to feel chilly. I looked down at my high heeled slippers, they weren't exactly the best footwear for walking around on lava rocks. Louette and I walk over to the campsite where David was sitting. I could tell by the look on his face, he was in shock and disbelief. I had known him for twenty-five years and although he wasn't blood, he was family. His older sister Doreen was married to my brother Bronson. Since David was ten years older than Kaleo, my son had always looked up to him. After Kaleo's accident, he renewed his interest in shoreline fishing something he and David had in common and one of the reasons for this weekend's camping trip. David had made all the arrangements for the permit.

Louette and I sat down with David. As he began telling us about their evening, I was so nervous I grabbed one of his cigarettes and lit it even though I had quit smoking a year ago. They had been eating dinner and talking when the Ulua fishing pole bell went off, they all ran across the plank to see what they caught, Alex ran back to the campsite to get the gaff for his brother but the fish got away. He took the gaff back to the campsite and came back to assist Kaleo in chumming the water and casting the fishing line back out into the ocean. Alex complained about a stomach ache and took his yellow dive light as he headed to the make shift bathroom they had.

David and Yuki were fishing right alongside the plank they had to cross to get back to land. The same area Yuki was suggesting

Alex might have fallen in but the waters were so rough that neither of them had heard anything. When Kaleo went to check on Al, he could not find him anywhere. Panic set in as they called out in the dark for Alex with no reply. David called his friends that lived in the area who immediately came and started looking for Al and they called 911. I asked David if he'd been to this side of the island before and he said he had been there a few times with his dad. I felt a little bit of relief knowing David was familiar with the place. Coming from Kawaihae, neither I, nor my sons had ever been here before. As David continued talking, I saw their dinner plates still with food on them. The coolers were full of fish they had speared for the wedding. Duke, Yuki and the girls were trying to keep warm.

I looked out to the surrounding area wishing I could see what was around me. I knew there was a blow hole because the water kept shooting out of it. We didn't dare wander too far from the camp because we were not familiar with the area and we didn't have good lighting. As the ocean began to calm down, I told Kaleo to go in the water in the area the current was pulling next to the plank to see if he could see anything. I knew he would do anything or go anywhere if it meant he would find Alex and bring him home safely. He didn't hesitate at all as he grabbed his dive mask and snorkel. As I watch him make his way across the plank with my brother Randy to the rock in the water, I was reminded that six months ago Kaleo was in the hospital with a broken neck and God healed him. I knew the same God who healed my oldest son was looking after Alex. I had to believe that and hold on to it. How could he heal one son and not care for my other son? I believed God was taking care of Al.

Around 2:30am, Randy walked with Kaleo to the rock in the water. We all watched from a distance from the cliff. We could see his light gliding through the water. His light shot to the surface, and he was screaming that he saw Al's light in the water. We were all crying. Thinking back now, I imagine Kaleo was too afraid to go any further afraid of what he may or may not find. Louette dialed 911 and told the operator we found Alexander's dive light in the water and that we think he fell in the ocean. The operator dispatched the Fire Department and assured Louette they were on their way back.

My twin cousins, Michael and Maitland, arrived around 4:00am in the morning. The news of what had happened spread through my family. Michael was doing all he could to reassure me that he would do everything possible to find Alex. Poor Maitland had worked a double shift, just to get home and hear the news then get back in his car and drive to the site with Michael. Maitland was so tired, he laid on the rocks and fell asleep. No one could do much of anything until the sun came up. Although my family is made up of divers, no one got in the water that night; the area was unfamiliar and we were all in shock. On that first night, when the rescue divers had been searching, they searched to the right of the plank. My husband dropped a water bottle in to see where the current was going and the current was pulling to the left side. That was the same side Kaleo had seen Al's light.

Finally, the sun came up and we could see where we were at. I was amazed at how crystal clear the blue ocean was and all the red fish I could see, it was as if I could just reach in the water and grab them with my hand. I thought about Alex and how amazed he must have been at the beautiful ocean. I realized I was standing on a cliff with the ocean about thirty feet below me. Soon I recognized my cousin Keola's boat out in the water along with other boats from Waimea. By this time there were many more trucks and boats arriving to help us look for Alex. Hawaii County Fire

Department's search and rescue team had also returned. A few of the homeowners from Kealakekua Bay knew something was going on because of the helicopter flying around the night before. They showed up as soon as the sun came up and asked if they could dive to help us. One of the local men familiar with the area arrived on his boat and offered to retrieve Al's light. Now the search started on the left side, going down the coastline and looking in the caves.

We sat there waiting for any word if they had found Alex. More and more people started making their way down to help us.

Waimea was about an hour and a half away. No matter how far away, family and friends continued to make their way down the mountain side to be with us. I stayed there for five days didn't think to bring anything clothes, blankets or food. But God provided everything we needed through our neighbors, friends, and family. They brought, clothes, food, cots and blankets. God made a way.

All of us were standing on the rocks looking into the ocean, praying Al would be found. The Fire Department Captain would report back to me that they hadn't seen him or found anything. The water around the rock where we suspected Alex to have fallen in was fifteen to twenty feet deep. About 100 yards out the ocean floor dropped off to 200 feet. The rescue divers were concerned that if Alex had drowned the current could have rolled him off the ledge.

Almost everyone was in shock that first day of searching. Many of Kaleo's friends along with our family and friends showed up to help with the search. Tyson Yoshizumi, Marke Sarme, Ronald Hayward, Willie Boy Akima, Arden Akau, they had families and jobs but had called in sick or taken the day off to help search for Al. They brought their fins and diving masks and began searching the waters with the rescue divers. Monday morning, my family got in the water and began looking—my husband, brothers, and cousins. One of the boats had a long rope that five or six divers would hold on too and the boat would pull them close to the ledge so they could look in that area.

Our Kahu (pastor), Billy Mitchell, also worked at Hualalai Resort. He came with a bunch of the beach boys on jet skis and boats to help dive and search the waters for Al. Leslie Gordon a local man from Kealakekua Bay was called by a friend's mom to assist in the search for Alexander. He showed up the second morning with his double haul glass bottom canoe. I got on the canoe with him as we went up and down the coastline looking through the glass bottom to see if I could see anything.

I would yell, "Alexander." "Alexander." "Alexander." I would do that in the daytime, I needed to do something, I needed to be looking for my son. When Kahu Billy saw me hollering for Al, he was so moved that the next day he brought the entire church, Mana Christian Ohana, to search and walk the coastline looking for Al; this was day three.

The outpouring of the community wanting to help was overwhelming. Lamar worked for one of the largest construction companies in Hawaii, Goodfellow Brothers Inc., they shut the whole job down to come search. All you saw were men with bright orange shirts walking down the coastline looking into every crack in those lave rocks, we looked everywhere, not a stone was unturned we had so many people searching for him.

Family as far as Kalapana on the East side of the island made their way to help in the search for Alex. Mahea's brother, Kainoa Hauanio, came with cousins and friends on jet skis. He would disappear in the water and be gone for minutes before flying up from the water to say, "Alex wasn't in that cave."

Then, he would go on to the next cave. The Fire Department's concern was growing more each day as numerous people showed up to help with the water and land search. The Fire Captain did not want anyone else to get hurt while searching for Al. He told me another boy had gone missing a few months earlier and the rescue party was nowhere near the size of our search party.

Even though God was my source of strength and I knew he had healed Kaleo only a few months before, I soon began reaching for any kind of help I could get. I had remembered one of Kaleo's aunties telling me she had spoken to a Filipino lady when Kaleo was in the hospital and this lady had said Kaleo would be okay. I called Kaleo's aunty and asked her to call the lady, a fortune teller, and ask her where Al was. She said Al was hurt and he was on a bed of grass. I had everyone searching, looking all over the terrain. Denise Freitas, a friend, and one of Al's favorite aunties called Kahu Billy and told him I was losing it. People were calling left and right saying Al was here or there and I was going all over the place listening to them Kahu Billy made the long journey from Waimea that night to come and pray with me. I knew what the bible said, but I was doing anything and everything I could to find Alex.

Hawaii County Fire Department mandate was to search for three days yet they extend the search to four days for Alexander. I remember sitting across the bay on a rock and crying. The fire captain landed his helicopter and walked over to comfort me. He knew I was a mother who would do anything to find my son. On that last day Hawaii County Fire Department got permission to take us up in the helicopter, the water was crystal clear I was amazed at how you could see the bottom of the ocean from so high in the sky. I knew, as I scanned the water, the rescue personnel had done all they could to find my son Alexander. The time had finally come to call off the search. No one would stop looking until I said it was time to stop.

I had been the one who told Kaleo on the first night we arrived, if Al was not here, he was with God. When the sun rose Sunday, the first morning of searching, I remembered seeing a rainbow and a Hawaiian hawk circling the sky above me. I thought it had been a sign that Al would be found. A Hawaiian man later told me it was a sign that Al had crossed over.

The time had come to leave Keopuka and Alexander, knowing this made me sick to my stomach, I could barely get off my cot that morning As I sat up, immediately the Lord spoke to me through His word. "Trust in the Lord with all your heart, lean not on your own understanding in all your ways. Shirley, acknowledge me and I will make your way straight." (Proverbs 3:5-6 NIV, with "Shirley" added for personalization.) For the first time in my life, I quoted a scripture and understood it. I poured out all my feelings to God and that was it for me. He was all I had; my hope was in Him.

As we drove up the mountain side away from the campsite, I couldn't stop crying knowing I was leaving Alexander behind; we never found his body. My son Kaleo was in the truck in front of us I worried for him and felt so much love for him. I knew he blamed himself, he tried so hard to find Al, we all did. "Please, Lord, be with Kaleo." I whispered softly.

Two weeks after losing Alexander, Kaleo and Mahea celebrated their wedding; a chair was decorated in memory of Alex and we honored him with the lighting of a candle and a moment of silence. For the next six months, Lamar and I spent every night crying. I would fall asleep holding on to my bible. God was gracious and gave me dreams immediately about Alex, one stood out the most. In my dream, the phone rang and when I answered it

Alex was on the other end. I was so happy to hear his voice and ask him if he was okay.

"Yes." he replied then went on to tell me, "Remember that lady from Church, remember her face, you should see her here she's all good."

He was always so very observant and curious. An elderly lady who sat in the front row at church had passed away a few months before, the kids would line along the wall in the front during praise and worship and I imagine Alex would stare at her wondering why she looked so frail. "Nothing dies up here, Mom. Here, everything is alive."

That was just one of many dreams I had of Alexander, the Lord knew my pain and comforted me with happy dreams of Alex. This brough me some comfort but I still had a question nagging at my soul. After Alex died, I came across a scripture in my quite time, Psalm 121:3, "He will not let your foot slip—he who watches over you will not slumber." (NIV)

This tormented me for a while. I kept wondering what had happened with Al if this scripture was true. On November 1, 2005, I finally asked God the nagging question, "Father, I am only going to ask you one time…why did this happen to Alex?"

That morning during my devotions he answered me. I opened my bible and it fell to Hebrews 11:5. The scripture said, "By faith Enoch was taken from this life, so that he did not experience death: "He could not be found, because God had taken him away." For before he was taken, he was commended as one who pleased God."" (NIV)

In that moment, I knew the Lord had answered my prayers. Alex had not suffered; God had taken him and this brought me great peace. I chose to praise God in the storm. I knew, with all my heart, the God who loved me and healed Kaleo, had Alex wrapped in his arms and was taking care of him until I could hold him again. Being grounded in Christ, is how I found peace, the kind of peace that surpassed all understanding. The world does not know this peace. But if Jesus has gone from your head to your heart, you're able to find peace even in the greatest of tragedies.

Chapter 7:

From Mountaintop to Valley Low Overnight

*A*ny parent who has been through the loss of a child will tell you it is not something you ever fully recover from. For as long as I breathe, I will grieve and ache and love my son Alexander with all my heart and soul. There will never come a time I won't think about who he would have been, or what he would have looked like. Watching students graduate from High School and College is bittersweet realizing my son will never experience that milestone. Seeing a family having fun and wondering what kind of family my son might have had when he grew up if he had been given the chance. There will always be a hole in my heart the size and shape of Alexander. Nothing will ever change that. Both the love and the pain I will always carry for him is immeasurable. I fully understand why some people can turn to alcohol or other substances to numb away the awful pain of loss. It is unbearable, a pain for me that only God could heal.

When we lost Alexander, I believe a part of my husband went with him. Each of us deals with loss in our own way. While we did take some time off, halting life permanently was not an option. We still had Auwae and Duke to raise, jobs to attend and bills to be paid. Then in 2007, life changed once again in a very drastic way when I lost my job.

I know jobs come and go but this came as quite a shock. When I was younger, going to school, working part-time, hanging at the beach were daily routines. There was no talk of college when I got to my senior year of high school. Whenever my dad brought up the subject, I would say, "Why can't you just be happy that I'm happy."

Who needed college? I was glad to be out of high school. By the time I was a junior in high school I had accumulated all the necessary credits to graduate which allowed for my senior year to consist of one class a day. School was over for me by 10:30am and off to work I went.

I got pregnant with Kaleo when I was nineteen and became a mom when I was twenty. I can't say I was ready to be a mother but I was happy to become one. I had always wanted to be like my mother with a house full of kids. As I explained earlier, things didn't work out between me and Kaleo's father, so I was a single mother for quite some time. Then, I met Lamar De Rego. We had Auwae and shortly after got married; all within a year of meeting him. Soon after, we had Alexander followed then Duke. Lamar got a job in the construction industry and I stayed home with the kids for seven years. I figured this would be what my life would look like for a while and I was okay with that, what I never imagined was the financial burden it would place on Lamar. He wanted me to start a daycare business, but after watching my own babies every day I could not imagine watching someone else's. I prayed and asked God to open the door for me to go back to work. I thought maybe I could go back and work at the hotel in the evening as a hostess knowing my cocktail waitress days were over. But I suppose God wanted me to grow beyond my comfort zone.

My older brother Bronson had a car washing business. One day he was washing a car for a lady who had moved to our town and started a mortgage company. He called to tell me she was looking for a receptionist to answer phones for two weeks. I had three kids under the age of six at the time and couldn't work full-time, but I thought, "Two weeks? Maybe I can swing that?"

Around the same time, Lamar was laid off for two weeks so I was able to go to work for those two weeks not worrying about what to do with the boys. God was orchestrating what would become my career for the next twenty years.

The two weeks ended and the assistance to the owner of the company wanted me to stay on full-time, but with three kids needing a babysitter for me to go to work, it didn't add up financially. I'd be working just to pay a babysitter. I figured I had to stay home with my kids. This was in April and by December she offered me a job. God knew we needed the extra money and Lamar reminded me every day I needed to contribute financially; God answered my prayers. Thankfully, I was able to qualify for a state funded program "First to Work". I found a daycare that participated in the program and gladly accepted the job.

Island Community Lending Mortgage was brand new to our town and the first mortgage broker of its kind on our island. The owner Marcelle Estes (Loren) had been well established on Oahu. My first day of work I thought I was to be the receptionist but Marcelle told me I was going to learn the mortgage business. I would be an assistant to another woman in the office. I started on a Wednesday and the next day, the woman I was hired to assist, got into an argument with another woman in the office and quit. I was in disbelief; it was only day two on the job for me. I called Lamar and told him I was pretty sure I had just lost my job as well.

To my surprise, Marcelle came into the office on Monday and said, "We're going to keep Shirley, but we do not train."

I don't know if maybe she thought I would quit once I realized I was in over my head but I didn't. Instead, I sought God. Every morning before I left for work, I prayed, "God, please help me understand what I am doing and what I am reading. Help me not be rude to the people who are rude to me on the phone."

This was such unfamiliar territory for me, I couldn't type; I didn't even know how to turn on a computer. One day I asked my co-worker who sat behind me, how to turn the computer on and she announced really loud, "Oh, you don't know how to turn on the computer?"

I wanted to hide under my desk. I know Marcelle had heard.

Our God, he is faithful to those who seek him. Little by little the Lord helped me understand what I was doing. In a year's time, I became Marcelle's assistant. She was a brilliant business woman but lacked people skill which made us a great team. People skills, I could handle! Almost every person who walked into the office knew me; and if they didn't, I made them feel welcomed. A year later they hired a girl from an escrow company whose expertise in closing mortgage transaction was highly sought after, I finally got the training I never received, although she had escrow experience, she needed to understand the loan process and Marcelle provided training to the whole office. Marcelle referred to me in the training sessions one day as being "unique" in how well I had caught on to the mortgage industry. I quietly sat there and gave all glory to God. Knowing I had prayed every day for His help and understanding, and he never let me down.

I stand by my words even today. I went from cutting up scrap paper and making copies to becoming a branch manager in the industry. God had taught me all I needed to succeed, I worked hard and applied myself to learning, I worked for Island Community Lending Mortgage for two years before I was offered a processor position with Charter Funding. The Hawaii Regional Vice President of Charter Funding, David Quandt, approached me one day asking me to consider becoming a Loan Officer. A loan officer was paid commission. I just couldn't, I needed my consistent salary every month. Many of Lamar and my arguments were because of money, I needed to count on that steady salary. Then David showed me a printout of all the loans that closed the previous month that were direct referrals from me and what that loan officer was paid. I still was not sure, but I took that leap of faith and I never looked back. God had always provided for me. The word of God tells us, "Do not despise the days of small beginnings." (Zechariah 4:10)

My small beginnings began at Island Community Lending in an environment that was not always friendly or helpful, but God allowed me, through his Holy Spirit, as only He can do, to learn and develop the skills I would need for this new season of my life.

The bible tells us numerous times how God will provide for all that we need. Sometimes, the provision comes in the form of those you are surrounded by and what they can teach you. I will never forgot, sitting across my desk one day from my customer as we went over her paperwork and she said, "Wow, you must have spent many years in college to learn all of this."

I looked at her and smiled. If she only knew; God was my teacher. He opened the right doors, put me in the right places, answered my prayers and I thanked Him for the success and the wonderful career he allowed me to experience. Three years into working for Charter Funding I was offered the Branch Managers position. The pay was very good I found myself making more money than I ever thought I would. Life at home was peaceful because I was now paying all the bills.

At twelve years old, Auwae was accepted and enrolled at Kamehameha Schools Kapalama Campus, a private school on the island of Oahu. He was missing home and having a hard time adjusting to boarding life. I wanted him to come home and be with us. I missed him and knowing he was struggling just broke my heart. Since Kamehameha Schools had an East Hawaii campus on our island, I bought a home near that campus and was planning to transfer Auwae so he would be closer to family. But he started playing sports and didn't want to come back anymore, I often think his dorm adviser had a lot to do with him changing his mind, they were always so good to him. I rented out the home to families who had kids going to Kamehameha Schools East Hawaii Campus

During the seven years I had been a stay-at-home mom, my life had been hell any time I had to ask my husband for money to buy something. Now that I had a very good job, his money was his own. I paid for our home, the rental home, and the new house we were building. Auwae's school tuition was paid for and there were no fights about money. If I wanted to get something, I had the freedom to go get it. I helped my mom with whatever she needed and anyone else that I could. I'm sure there were times I gave a little more than I should have but I was happy to help.

Then, on August 16th 2007, my manager called me on the phone and said, "Shirley we are filing bankruptcy, the branch is closing tomorrow."

I knew the mortgage industry as a whole was in turmoil since it was all over the news, but my manager kept assuring us we were fine. Just like that, I went from earning a six-figure salary to nothing, overnight. I don't know that anyone can prepare for something like that. When I called Lamar and told him what was happening, he said, "Good one, Shirley."

I said, "What do you mean, it isn't my fault."

He blamed me for the branch closing, his response had hurt. I was scared, I had three mortgages, a truck payment, Auwae's school tuition. Back then, there was no such thing such as loan modifications; mortgage companies couldn't help me. I tried to stay afloat by taking money from my retirement fund and kids' college funds. I lost my house in Hilo to foreclosure, then lost another home. Lamar was paying all the household bills and God was providing a little here and a little there, tension started building again between Lamar and I as he was back paying the bulk of the bills. but we still did not have enough to keep everything. I knew God was with me, I knew his word said "never will I leave you or forsake you." (Hebrews 13:5) I knew he cared and would see me through. God was my only hope, but it was certainly a very deep valley.

Chapter 8:

Then Came the Plague

The employees from my old company stuck together for quite some time. Most of us, went to work for another company in the industry, there were daily challenges as mortgage guidelines and mortgage products were eliminated, new rules and regulations were established it was definitely a learning curve. One by one we each went to work for other companies who provided us better opportunities. While we were financially struggling, Lamar suggested Auwae should come home and attend public school. Paying for his tuition and boarding at the private school was well beyond our budget. Auwae had accomplished many things at Kamehameha School; excelling in both academics and basketball. He had come to love the school and since it was his senior year, I couldn't take that from him. My cousin Danny Akau lived a few miles from the school, so I asked him if Awuae could stay with him. This would allow Auwae to become a day student and we would no longer have to pay the boarding fee which made the tuition more affordable. I'm glad he was able to continue on at the school he loved.

In September 2009, my life took another turn. While some might read that and picture a slight curve in the road, that's not what I mean when I say "a turn". For me, every turn in my life is like a switchback on a 70MPH roller coaster. Things are going along just fine and then suddenly…sharp, hard turn in a new direction.

I've always loved wearing high heel shoes and slippers (sandals, as some might call them). Even in school, I didn't care if they made me taller than the boys, I would still wear heels. One night, while I was getting ready for bed, I massaged my foot and felt a lump. I told my husband about it and he said I should be sure to get it checked out. When I finally got it checked out, my doctor said it was nothing and suggested I see a foot doctor. She thought it was probably from wearing high heel shoes all my life. As she looked at my chart, she noticed I hadn't had a mammogram. Since I was forty-nine already and had never had one, she asked if I would like to schedule one. She gave me a paper for a blood test and another one to schedule a mammogram. I misunderstood her thinking they were going to call me. Every few weeks, I would clean out my purse and run across that paper. I'd think, "Why haven't they called me yet?"

But instead of calling them to find out, I would shove it back into my purse. Finally, the third time I found the paper, I crumbled it up and threw it away. Not long after I threw the paper away, I started getting coughing fits at night. They went on for about a week before my husband said I needed to go see the doctor. I went to see my doctor and asked if I could get antibiotics. She told me they weren't needed as I was already over the worst of it. Then she asked why I hadn't scheduled my mammogram yet. Nine months had passed since she had initially told me to schedule it.

Since, it was all within the same building, she gave me the paper and told me to go straight down to schedule it; which I did. I took the mammogram and went back to life. I had no idea; God was orchestrating these things. The lump in my foot and coughing fits had both lead me to the doctor and there was a bigger reason for this.

A week after the mammogram, I received a call from the hospital. They wanted me to come the next day for a follow-up mammogram. I asked her if there was a problem because this didn't seem normal but she assured me it was probably nothing and sometimes you just have to take another one. I knew that was probably not the case and had a bad feeling. They wouldn't suggest I come in the very next day for another test unless there was something wrong. My mother and sister, Lana, were with me and when I hung up the phone I began crying. Lana prayed over me.

After the mammogram, an appointment was scheduled with my doctor to go over the results. Dr. Perlas walked into the examination room and told me they had found two lumps in my left breast. She would schedule an ultrasound and a biopsy. I would have results back in three days. I remember walking out of her office saying to myself this is just another opportunity for God to work, believing test results would be fine. During this time, my mother was also experiencing health issues so I tried to focus on her and not think too much about these tests. On the fourth day Dr. Perlas' office called to tell me my test results were back and schedule my appointment to see her. Mom had an appointment that morning as well in the same medical building. Her heart specialist was right across the hallway from Dr. Perlas' office, so I left her there with my cousin while I went to get my results. We planned to eat lunch afterwards.

When Dr. Perlas walked in, she told me she was surprised she hadn't heard from me. Usually, her phone would be ringing off the hook when someone was waiting on results.

I smiled and said, "I'm just believing it is benign and all is well."

She said, "Shirley, the biopsy came back malignant; you have cancer."

I left her office and my cousin was pushing my mom in her wheelchair to me. I wheeled her out to the van and as I was helping her in, she said, "How did everything go, Shirley?"

The news hadn't quite set in all the way. All I could think about was not worrying my mother and getting back to my house. I calmly replied, "Oh it went well, mom, I have cancer."

We didn't go to lunch because I was no longer hungry. Instead, I dropped her and my cousin off and returned home. My older brother, Bronson, was spending the weekend at my home recovering from a surgery. I went to my bedroom, buried my head in a pillow and began crying, "Why is this happening to me?"

Bronson opened my door and said, "Don't cry, Shirley, God can heal you. He is the great physician." My family had known about the mammogram and the possibility of cancer, my tears confirmed what my brother now knew was true.

I felt so violated. Receiving this news from the doctor reminded me of the time I was at my son's ballgame and ran to get something from the car. Someone had broken into my car and stolen my shopping bags and briefcase. I felt so violated and this felt the same only it was my own body. Why had this happened?

Duke had a football game later that night in Hilo. As much as I wanted to stay in my bed forever, I needed to get up and get ready to go to the game. I caught a ride to the game so Lamar and I could ride home together; he was working in Hilo. We both pulled up at the same time at Hilo Stadium. I walked over to Lamar as he was getting out of his truck and said, "The test results were malignant, I have cancer."

"How the hell did you get that, Shirley?"

His reply was gut-wrenching. I felt abandoned by the one person I wanted to be there for me. I tried my best to concentrate on the football game, but I was so preoccupied by the test results and Lamar's reaction. The drive home to Waimea was extra quiet, Lamar and I did not talk about anything important. I was grateful for Duke riding the bus back to school with the team because it gave me more time to figure out a way to tell him his mom had cancer.

The ultrasound had revealed nine lumps. The cancer was in the milk duct of my left breast and had broken up. Dr. Perlas referred me to Dr. Howard Wong general surgery specialist at North Hawaii Community Hospital in town. Dr. Wong said they would need do a lumpectomy; going into the side of my breast to remove it. But upon further investigation, he determined this would not be possible and they would have to remove my whole breast. At that point, I told him, "You might as well remove the other one also so I don't have to come back."

I wasn't bitter and didn't want to take any chances. He said that wouldn't be necessary or recommended. Since North Hawaii Community Hospital in Waimea was a small facility and not a big Medical Center like Queen Medical Center on Oahu I told him I was going to get a second opinion and get back with him. But after praying about it, I felt like God had given Dr. Wong all the wisdom he needed in this area and I should go forward with his recommendations. On October 5, 2009 I had a mastectomy.

When my family found out about my cancer, my sister Lana who had recently dedicated her life to Christ, told me she was going to put me on the prayer chain at her church. I said, "No you're not. Prayer chains can turn into gossip chains and I don't want people speaking death over me."

Then I found a book by Dodie Osteen. The first thing that caught my attention was a scripture from the book of James 5: 14-15 that said, "Is anyone among you sick? Let them call the elders of the church to pray over them and anoint them with oil in the name of the Lord. 15 And the prayer offered in faith will make the sick person well; the Lord will raise them up. If they have sinned, they will be forgiven." (NIV)

Dodie had been healed from liver cancer and searched scriptures to stand on her healing. I had never heard this scripture before. A week later reading another book on healing, the first thing that caught my eye was the scripture from James 5:14-15 on healing. I felt the Lord saying, "Shirley, how can I heal you if you don't let people pray for you?"

I called my sister, "Okay, put me on the prayer chain. And can you ask the elders to prayer over me and anoint me with oil because that is what it says in the bible."

Although I had been going to another church, I had recently started attending my sister's church. She was singing on the worship team and I wanted to support her; but I didn't have a relationship with the pastors at the church like she did so I thought it would be better if she asked them to pray for me.

The night before my surgery I asked the Lord to show me a sign that everything was going to be okay. The window in my bathroom faces beautiful Mauna Kea Mountain and since there are no houses around me, my window has no curtain. As I stepped out of the shower and looked out the window, I saw the biggest brightest moon and remembered something a friend had told me. "Shirley, the way God works is like the moon. Sometimes, we know he's there we can see and feel him working in our lives, everything is going well, and then there are time when we cannot see him or feel him and wonder if he cares or hears us, but like the moon on a dark night God is still there with us."

I was reminded of God's promise, ""Never will I leave you; never will I forsake you." (Hebrews 13:5b NIV)

Seeing this big, beautiful moon out my window felt like God reminding me everything would be okay. The next morning, as I was getting ready to leave for my appointment, Duke came into my room crying, scared for me. I walked him over to my bathroom window and pointed to the bright orange and yellow colors scattered across the sky from the sunrise. I said to him, "The same God who did that is taking care of your mommy."

Auwae who was in his first year of college in San Jose City College called me crying and asked to pray over me before I left for the hospital. Before getting prepped for surgery, I stopped by my mom's hospital room to see her. She was in there for her own health reason, and I wanted to stop by and reassure her everything would be all right. Well, there is also something comforting about seeing your mother right before a scary situation.

The nurses were talking about how handsome the new anesthesiologist who would be handling my surgery was. They started the drugs and began taking me to the operating room. I was looking around at the landscapes painted on the hallways saying, "Wow, it's so beautiful."

When I finally got to the operating room, I told the anesthesiologist all the nurses had been talking about how handsome he was. I'm sure the nurses appreciated my honesty. Dr. Wong asked if I had anything else to say. I asked if I could pray and BOOM, I was out.

After I woke up in recovery, Dr. Wong said I had made the right choice. I had a tumor against my chest wall and the only way to know for sure if it was a cancerous tumor was to remove my breast. The cancer was stage two but they had gotten everything. My hospital room looked like a flower shop because there were so many flowers and cards from friends and family wishing me well. The morning of my surgery, my husband had to fly to Maui for work. I had thought about calling his manager and asking why they would not let him get off work to be with me during my surgery but deep down I couldn't. I knew there was a good chance he hadn't even asked to take the time off and I would rather not know if he couldn't be there for me.

The day I was diagnosed with cancer was the end of our relationship. We continued to be married but there was no intimacy neither physical or emotional from that moment on. Going to doctor appointments alone while other women sat and waited with their husbands was very difficult. I rely on God and he gave me strength. My family, friends and co-workers poured in and filled that time and space with love for me. My older son, Kaleo, told me he would help me during my recovery time. This was very humbling for me because I was usually the one who was helping other people. I went through seven different operations for reconstructive surgery. All of these surgeries took place on Oahu and I was grateful for my family on Oahu—my stepdaughter Ululii and her husband Rob, my cousin Danny and his wife Lehua, who was a nurse.

Even though I did not have the support of the one person I desired to have support from, my husband; God brought support in from everywhere else. People from my previous church and new church brought groceries and meals every night. Friends and family surrounded me with love during my recoveries and God even brought in financial support.

Once the surgery to remove my breast and tumors were done, I was scheduled to see an oncologist, Dr. Desolvo. His recommendation was radiation and chemotherapy he said I had a 52% chance the cancer would return. Sitting in the exam room listening to him I felt in my spirit I was healed; I was standing on the scripture God had given me in James 5:13-14.

I told him, "Dr. Desolvo I believe I am healed."

He told me I could have a test done to determine if the treatments would not be necessary but my medical would not cover the cost of the $4,000 test. The choice was mine. I believed I was healed and opted for the test. God provided the money! I will never forget when Dr. Desolvo walked into the exam room a month later to deliver the good news, I did not need radiation or chemotherapy. My spirit was doing summersaults in me. I left his office and couldn't wait to call Lamar and the rest of my family to share the good news. The Lord provided the best care for me at North Hawaii Community Hospital. Our small-town medical staff was kind and professional. I believe God made doctors and nurses, as well as you and me, and He blessed them with their talent. God surrounded me with His best; I was, and still am, completely healed.

Chapter 9:

The Circle of Life

*L*ife is a circle; people are born and one day each of us will die. None of us want to think about when our final day might be. We all plan to live well into our eighties or nineties and maybe even make it to one hundred if we are really lucky. When we are kids, death seems like it is an eternity away. We never truly grasp how fragile and unpredictable life is until someone, we love, dies. Even then, although death becomes a reality, I don't know that we grasp what has happened.

Before I began my battle with cancer, my mother was battling her own health issues. There were many doctor appointments and many hospital stays. At one point she had fallen and broke her hip. Once she fully recovered for the fall, she had another fall. I remember the doctor telling us that we would need to bathe and clean our mother and I said, "No, I will not do that."

It wasn't that I would not care for my mother. I just could not see taking away her dignity and independence in that way. Mommy was always such a strong woman. However, all of us kids realized it was time to put a plan in place to take care of Mommy. I would start the day by arriving at her home at 6:30AM taking care of breakfast and medication. Duke caught the school bus right in front of her home every morning. Then at 10:30, my sister Lana would stay with her while I went to work. Then, Randy, who lived with our mother, would take over at 3:30PM and have her the rest of the night until I arrived the next morning. I think it was the hardest on Randy because mommy would always be calling out in the middle of the night for him and he worked so early in the morning.

I remember one morning while walking around the block, the Lord impressed on my heart to spend every moment I could with my mother because she wouldn't be here for much longer. On these morning walks, the Lord showed me the deep loneliness and depression she felt at times in her life. I understood now why 1 Corinthians 10:13 had been her life scripture. God's word was rooted in her spirit her source of strength and help in all those lonely times.

When I had my surgery, she told me that she was going to move in with me and take care of me. I said, "No, Mommy, someone needs to take care of you."

Since I could no longer physically care for my mother, Lana and Randy would now have the full responsibility of her daily care. She cried to me telling me how sorry she felt for Randy, she would call out five to six times a night for his help to go to the bathroom. He woke every morning at 3:30AM to leave for work, she worried about him driving and not having a good night's rest. I tried to do as much as I could for my mom but I knew she needed more help than we could offer.

The hardest decision I had to make was convincing her to go back to the Rehab Center. She had spent a few months at the facility when she recovered from hip surgery but they also offered a long-term care facility. I told her this would not be forever, she could utilize the twenty-four care until she got back on her feet, maybe a year or less. Then I could care for her in my home. She agreed to go and I settling her into her room at the facility. After leaving here, I cried all the way home. That was March 18, 2010.

The hospital was in walking distance from Duke's school so he would walk to the hospital after school and visit Grandma until I got there. We stayed with her until visiting hours were over.

On March 23, 2010, I remember it being a Tuesday, we were visiting my mom as we usually did—me, Duke, my brother Randy and his wife. She had finished dinner and we were getting ready to go. I walked up to her bed and said, "Okay, mommy, I'll see you tomorrow."

As I helped put her oxygen mask on, she said, "Goodbye, Shirley."

Her smile and tone felt very strange. "What? Where are you going?" I asked and laughed away the weird tone, "I'll see you tomorrow."

She said, "I might not be here tomorrow."

I said, "Oh, girl, you'll be here." I hugged my mom, gave her a kiss, and went home.

At 9PM, my brother Randy called me crying, the hospital had called and said mommy died. I was sitting on the couch watching a show with Kaleo and his wife, Lamar had just gone to the room to get ready for bed. I started to wail and cry hoping Lamar would come back out and see what was wrong. When I went to the room to tell Lamar my mother had died, he lay on the bed with his eyes closed.

Kaleo said, "Come on, mom, Duke and I will take you to the hospital."

Auwae was at the University of Arizona. My brother Bronson had called him to tell him Grandma died, he handed me the phone Auwae was crying. He couldn't believe his father was not there for me and told me he would be home in the morning.

Even amongst my own pain, I always made excuses for my husband. I knew his behavior was not what it should be but I would tell the boys he had a difficult life. This was true, but I cannot imagine what I was teaching them by normalizing his emotional disconnect. Once again, I pushed aside my feelings of abandonment and leaned into God.

Mommy had been such a significant person in my life, I know many people feel the same about their mothers. She was always there for us; showing love and support. She wasn't perfect, is there any mom who is, but she was perfect for me. I knew she had faults but I loved my mother so much. There was so much she had gone through, so many things I had learned from watching her, and now I would not see her again until my time on earth was through.

There was a bittersweet comfort in thinking about her and Alex hugging together in heaven. Two people I loved would no longer be present to love on or hold tight. Thinking on this brought with it the reality that our days on earth are not promised, not a single one. I imagine even if we live eighty or ninety years, it will all seem as if a short moment compared to the eternity which awaits us.

Chapter 10:

My Heart Can Bear No More

*A*t the beginning of the book, I mentioned how my mother would always tell me, "Shirley, God will not give you more than you can bear."

This scripture (1 Corinthians 10:13) is widely misquoted as it actually says he will not give you more than you can bear without giving you a way out. I could have been tempted to succumb to deep depression when Kaleo broke his neck and even more so when Alex died but instead, I trusted in God. The same could have happened when I lost my job, got diagnosed with cancer, and lost my mother. Each time, I chose to press in to God and trust him more. This isn't to say anything about the person that I am. I wouldn't say there is anything special about me but instead I would go to say God can be whatever you need whenever you need it. He will bring peace amongst the worst chaos. He will bring comfort to an aching soul. He will restore your joy when you've suffered a deep sense of hopelessness. God can, and will, be whatever we need whenever we need it. The most amazing thing is that all we have to do is put our faith in him. No special tricks or gimmicks just trust in him.

Knowing this, and living through situations where he has provided, does not make it any easier to turn to him when the waves come crashing back down on your soul. It is still a choice we must chose to make on our own.

"No temptation has overtaken you except what is common to mankind. And God is faithful; he will not let you be tempted beyond what you can bear. But when you are tempted, he will also provide a way out so that you can endure it." 1 Corinthians 10:13 NIV

Bronson Duke Nanoa De Rego, or "Dukie" as we liked to call him, was my little opihi. Opihi are like the escargot of Hawaiian; little shell urchins that stick to rocks. If you touch one of these, they suction their self to the rock so hard it is almost impossible to get them off. Duke was my opihi, he stuck by my side closer than any of his brothers. I was nineteen when I had Kaleo and thirty-five when I had Duke. We really weren't planning on having any more children when I got pregnant with him. With Auwae and Alex, we found out they were going to be boys but with Duke we decided to wait until the baby was born. The whole pregnancy I thought maybe it would be a girl because it felt different than my other pregnancies; but along came Duke and that was okay.

Alex and Duke were almost night and day. Alex was aggressive and Duke was passive. Duke was the teddy bear of the family so big and loveable but nobody was ever allowed to call him fat. Whenever we went to the beach, he would always wear a t-shirt and he was unable to play pop warner football because he exceeded the weight limit. I knew Duke struggled with accepting his weight and I never wanted it to be an issue for him.

Even though I worried, none of this stopped Duke. He loved playing baseball. His dad was his coach and Duke knew that if he didn't hit the ball far enough, Lamar would put someone in to run the bases for him. This motivated Duke to hit home runs every single time he was up to bat because he didn't want anybody running bases for him. Unlike his brothers, Duke never ventured very far from home. He enjoyed spending time with me and being around the house.

The first time he ever ventured outside of our family was when his eighth-grade class took a trip to the east coast. For Christmas that was my gift for him. In the upcoming year both him and Auwae would be traveling to the east coast. Duke for school and Auwae for basketball. I was so nervous for Duke. Auwae had been living away from home boarding at Kamehameha School on Oahu for quite some time but this was a big deal for Duke. I wasn't sure he was ready for this. He would be sharing a hotel room with other boys and I was so nervous they might say something about his weight; but that never happened. He went to Washington D.C., visited New York Times Square, and saw a play. He had the best time on this trip.

To raise money for the trip, the school had an imu, (underground oven) you bought a pan and filled it with your favorite dish, it was cooked overnight in the imu. Duke was so excited to help with the fundraiser because when he grew up, he wanted to be a pig farmer like Lamar's father, his grandfather. He even had plans to help on the pig farm during the summer.

Because of his size, there were times when Duke would get picked on at school. Lucky for him, his brother Kaleo was into Jiu Jitsu and boxing. So, I had all of the boys take boxing lessons during the summer. I wanted to make sure they were able to defend themselves, especially Auwae who was all alone on another island. Even though he wasn't very fast, Duke loved boxing with his brothers. My garage was the Jiu Jitsu gym and there would be times when Duke would come into the house complaining about what Kaleo was making him do. As soon as Kaleo would holler his name, he would wipe his eyes and run back out to the garage. He certainly was the baby of the family and I was perfectly fine with this. I loved having a mama's boy.

My boys all played sports growing up, Kaleo played every sport—football, baseball, basketball, soccer, boxing, surfing, motocross—you name it he played it. Jiu Jitsu became a passion he pursued as he got older and continues today. Auwae loved basketball from the minute he could dribble a ball. His team won the Hawaii State High School Basketball Championship in his senior year at Kamehameha School Kapalama Campus. This was a very proud moment for our family. Even though he loved basketball, ironically, he received a scholarship to play football with the University of Arizona. Alexander wanted to be like his older brother Kaleo, he played basketball, baseball and football. Before every game, Alex would tell me I would have to pay him five dollars every time I yelled his name; then after the game he would come up to me and say, "That's fifteen dollars."

Duke on the other hand lit up with pride every time I yelled from the sidelines to cheer him on. He had always tagged along to all of Auwae and Alex's games but this was his time to shine. Nineth grade was his first opportunity to try out for football and he was very excited to make the team. I remember being so nervous about him having to get into the tight uniform being so self-conscious about his body. All those worries went away when I watched my football player step onto the field with confidence, he was finally growing into his skin. Nineth grade seemed to be his year to shine.

The school year was coming to an end and Memorial Day weekend was upon us. Although he usually liked to stay at home and be around family, he wanted to get out and do something with friends but nothing seemed to be working. When Monday rolled around, I was watching my granddaughter, Lili. One of Duke's friends asked if Duke could go with them to Kona. They had to get a tire for his mom's car and I'm sure he wanted some company for the trip.

When Alex had asked to go camping, Lamar had told him he could not go. Then, when he begged me the next morning, I caved in and allowed him to go. After that experience, I never wanted to be the one to give permission. The few times Duke would ask to go out, I would always tell him to ask Lamar. This day, he came back into the house and said, "Dad, said to ask you."

I told him that would be fine and gave him some money to buy pizza while they were at Costco. He left for Kona earlier in the morning and as the day went on, I began to wonder where Duke was. I didn't have his friend's number but I knew of a few people I could try to get it from. I decided to finish watching the movie with my granddaughter and vacuum before I started tracking Duke down.

My phone rang and the girl on the line said, "Auntie, this is Faith. Dukie fell." I couldn't quite make out what she was saying and thought she had said Duke fell off a go kart. When I repeated back what I thought she had said, she replied, "No, Dukie fell off a golf cart."

I said, "Is he okay?"

When she told me her dad was giving him CPR I screamed and asked where they were. She told me they were at her on Mana

Road by her grandma's home. I yelled for Lamar. "Something's wrong with Duke."

Lamar immediately left, I could not get up off the floor I was crying and pleading with God to let Dukie be okay and my grand-daughter started to cry. A friend Ala Lindsey who came upon the accident rushed to our house to tell us something had happened to Duke. I told him Lamar was already on his way to the accident. When Lamar got there, the paramedic was performing CPR on Duke.

Lamar came back to the house as the paramedics took Duke. He told me to get dressed so we could go to the hospital. All I could say was, "I can't do this again. Please father give me the strength."

Lamar began yelling at me to get dressed, "We need to go, Shirley."

I called Kaleo and told him what had happened. I needed him to meet us at the hospital and needed someone to take Lili.

Duke was in a drug induced coma by the time we arrived. The doctors had taken this measure because of his head injury. When I heard this, I fell to the ground crying. Duke was scheduled to be air lifted to Queens Medical Center on Oahu one of us had to go with him. At that point, I could see it in their faces. Every person at the hospital, knew what was wrong with Duke but no one could say it. Their goal was to stabilize him and get him to Oahu. I could not believe I was here in this place of uncertainty with another child. When the doctor told me Duke would be taken to Oahu and they would hopefully see what could be done; I clung to that. There was hope? Okay, I was going to pray for his healing. He would come out of this.

There were a lot of emotions in the hospital that day. I hadn't realized they put Duke on life support until I walked into his room and realized he couldn't breathe on his own. The air flight arrived quickly, no long delay like there had been with Kaleo. Sadly, with all the machines needed to keep him alive, they decided Duke would have to make the trip alone. There wouldn't be room for anyone to fly with him.

My older brother was so upset he began yelling at Faith's father. Duke was the jewel of the family. He was always respectful, kind and helpful to everyone. We were all in shock that this had happened to him. Faith was crying and kept apologizing, "I'm so sorry, Auntie, I was driving too fast. It's all my fault."

I told her we just needed to pray for her friend; for Dukie. Kahu Billy Mitchell showed up and his look of disbelief said it all. Neither of us could imagine we would ever be in this place again under such circumstances. As soon as they loaded Duke into the ambulance, we all jumped into our cars and followed them to the air pad. It was a short five-minute drive from the hospital and we all piled out of the cars and began praying. Duke's friend, Austin, the boy who had invited him to Kona, could not stop crying. I asked for everyone to lay hands on Austin and pray for him as well. When Alex was lost at sea, I saw how feeling responsible had taken a toll on Kaleo. I didn't want Austin to feel, in any way, this was his fault.

We could not get out on any commercial flight until 7AM the next morning. Duke's older sister Ululii and my cousin Danny planned to meet him at the hospital and stay with him until I arrived the next morning.

When we got back to the house, Lamar retreated to the bedroom and went to bed. This was so much different from when we had lost Alex. Back then, we were scared and grieving together, clinging on to one another. Being diagnosed with cancer had caused a giant unrepairable rift between us.

Kaleo was in the process of moving back home. He was in between trips when I told him something had happened with Duke and I needed him to meet me at the hospital. Auwae was away at college. His friend's mother worked for United Airlines and they put him on the next flight home. As much as Lamar and I had gone through, our kids Kaleo, Auwae and Ululii had been through the same. Each of us facing these difficult life situations and each of us navigating through them in our own ways.

Driving to Hilo Airport the next morning, I noticed as the sun was rising in the sky, there was an orange and yellow cloud formation which looked like the silhouette of a child's face. I looked at it and thought, "Is this a sign Duke is not in this life anymore?"

I dismissed the thought and committed not to stop praying for his healing. Arriving at the hospital Duke looked like he was asleep and at peace; he was on life support. The Neurologist came into the room. He took me and Lamar into a side room and explained that Duke had hit his head so hard it cracked his skull. His brain had expanded and was pushing on his skull. They had drilled a hole in the skull in hopes to alleviate the swelling.

Queen's Medical Center Critical Care Unit only allowed for patients to have two visitors at a time. Family and friends started pouring into the hospital. Ululii had been with Duke all night with her brother. I knew she needed to go home and take care of her babies and reassured her we would all be here when she returned. Auwae arrived and I felt so heartbroken for him. He was always away from home during every tragedy our family had endured. I hugged him as he cried for Dukie's condition. I realized as I held Auwae how much I had missed seeing him. My niece Dayna arrived from California. She was the cool cousin the boys have always loved. Her father, my brother Bronson, was comforting her. My whole family was once again gathered together under such tragic circumstances. My brother Bronson with his wife Doreen along with their son and daughter—Alika and Dayna. My sister Lana. My brother Randy with his wife Desiree, with their daughter Nelly and their sons, Christepher and Chace. Our Church, Mana Christian Ohana, has paid for all my family to be here with me. When Kaleo arrived with Mahealani and Lili, he noticed Duke was in the same room he was in when he was here for his neck injury.

Here we are again, another son, another injury, how can this be happening to me Lord? Why is this happening to me again?

Although the visitor limit was two people, the hospital allowed us to have whomever we wanted in Duke's room. At one point, I think there were twenty people in the room. Every day we were praying singing and worshiping in his room. We took turns sleeping in the room with him so he would not be alone. Dayna, Auwae and Kaleo took the first night. I took the second night with Lamar and Ululii. The waiting room was overflowing with friends and family who got a call about Duke and came to the hospital to pray with us. Churches on Oahu heard and sent their pastors to pray with us.

One of the ladies who had come with a church to pray for Duke, an attractive Hawaiian woman with red lipstick, looked at me just outside Duke's room and said, "It is hard to touch the face of God and want to come back."

This encounter became a memory I will never forget. I understood what she was saying. I believed God gave Duke the decision to stay with him or come back and Duke chose to stay. This was a difficult thing to wrap my head around. I knew inside of me Duke had left this earth on the day of his accident, but accepting it was a whole other story. I cried by his bed and begged him to come back to us. I told him I would do whatever I had to do to take care of him. Three days went by and the doctor asked us if we would consider organ donation. Duke was clinically brain dead.

I hadn't even thought about such a thing but found out Lamar, Kaleo and Auwae were all organ donors. I had to think about it for a moment because I was not. Eventually, I decided it was what Duke would have wanted. Dukie always wanted to help other people so I agreed to allow his organs to be donated as long as they all went to people in Hawaii. On June 3rd 2010, my son, Bronson Duke Nainoa De Rego, died. He became a hero that day as his organs gave life to three men and sight to two women.

Chapter 11:

Turning Sorrows to Joy

*L*osing Duke was a huge test of my faith. I struggled with it so deeply. Not only because of the son I had lost but also because of the friend I had lost. Duke loved spending time with me and he was always there. Kaleo was out of the house, Alex was gone, Auwae was at college, and Lamar was no longer there emotionally; but Duke was right by my side. We got through Alex's death together, he stayed by me during my breast cancer, and we grieved the loss of my mother together. Duke was my little opihi and now he was gone.

Did I question God? Of course, I did. I'm not sure I know a human who wouldn't. This didn't mean that I ever lost trust in God, it simply meant I could not understand. Why would he allow one son to experience total healing, another to be lost at sea, and another to die in an accident? I know God knew my pain but, to make matters worse, Satan also knew my pain.

I had my moment of questioning when we lost Al and the same happened after Duke died. I would question God about his word I had spoken over Duke; "Honor thy mother and thy father and all will go well with you." I had told Duke this all the time and wanted to know, "What happened, Lord?"

Duke was the most respectful kid I knew. He honored me and Lamar so much yet he didn't get to experience a full life on earth?

What was going on? None of it seemed fair in any way. On top of this, I was upset at Duke for choosing to leave me. I had promised him over and over that I would take care of him but he still chose to go to heaven. He chose heaven over me and that hurt my heart so badly. God knew the loneliness, the pain and anguish I was experiencing. I searched his word for comfort but continued feeling broken. God knew my pain and blessed me with a dream to bring me the comfort I needed. Just as he had done with Alex.

"Children, obey your parents in the Lord, for this is right. "Honor your father and mother"— which is the first commandment with a promise— "so that it may go well with you and that you may enjoy long life on the earth.""
Ephesians 6:1-3 NIV

This dream was a year after Duke's death. In the dream, I had returned to my childhood home, I was returning from work and for some reason was planning to see my father at the radio station. Mommy was in her room and I asked her if she was going with me to see Dad.

"No." she repleid.

I leaned in, grabbed her face and kissed her. "I love you, Mommy."

Although my eyes were closed I could see a bright white light. Then from the top of my head to the soles of my feet, I felt this warmth, this peace, pour over my whole body like oil pouring over me. A presence of love I have never felt before, a kind of love we don't feel here on earth. The closes I think we get to this love is the way we feel at the birth of a child or the day we are married. It was a love that no one, or nothing, could take away.

At that moment God said, "Shirley, this is what Duke, your mom, and Alex feel in my presence. Nothing else exits but my love."

On earth, we come close to that love, but it is immediately taken away by anger or fear. In God's presence, it is all our loved ones in eternity will ever know. God provided me the peace I was looking for to let Dukie go. God is so good, he knew my heart broke after losing Alex and shattered with Duke, he provided the comfort that only he knew would heal it.

After this dream, I forgave Duke for choosing Heaven over me. I hadn't even realize I was holding on to unforgiveness regarding his death. Jesus set me free through his love.

When Alex died, I remember the most important thing to me from that point on was to be good, do good and live a good life. All I could think about was getting to heaven and seeing my son again. Until one day Jesus convicted me by saying, "What about me?"

Jesus had paid the price with his life for me and my children; because of his sacrifice, they were both with him. I started crying and asked for his forgiveness after recognizing I was putting my son before God. God knew my heart. He knew the pain I was going through and he was patient with me during my loss. I am so thankful he allows us room to grow and mature in our faith.

I started living my life and giving it all for the kingdom. I wanted to see Jesus face to face one day. Once again, God showed patience with me when he asked, "Do you think anybody else might want to see me in Heaven?"

Oh yeah, that was true. He died for everyone not just me.

Something I have come to realize over the years is that when we hand our pain over to God, he will repurpose it into something amazing and beautiful—weeping and sorrow to joy, ashes to beauty. His word promises this to us.

In April of 2011 almost a year after Duke died, we had the opportunity to meet the people who had received Duke's organs. Every year, Hawaii Legacy of Life hosts a ceremony for donor families, when we agreed Duke would become a donor, they promised me in the hospital I would be able to meet his donors. It is hard to explain what I felt as I sat at the ceremony. Part of me felt like Duke himself would walk through the door. Instead, two gentlemen who looked nothing like Duke walked in—an African American man who had received Duke's liver and a Filipino man who had received Duke's kidney. Once they sat down and we all started talking we were overwhelmed with joy to hear their stories. Jerry Brown, the liver recipient, was born in October and a momma's boy just like Duke. He served in the military for thirty years and had recently retired. He had been on his way to see his mother in Florida—expecting it to be his last visit before he died—when he received the call regarding the organ donation. He still called his mom every day.

Junior Eders, the kidney recipient, was also born in October like Duke. He had a wife and a daughter who loved to travel but because of his dialysis, three days a week, he didn't travel with them; now he could. He asked me if Duke liked fish. I said, "Duke loved food!!"

Junior said he did not like fish but since receiving Duke's kidney he had to eat fish at least once a week. We all laughed and cried. Ululii said they were now just brothers from a different mother. We all got a good laugh out of this. Duke was living on. We were all so grateful to see God take something so tragic and work it out for good in the lives of others. We have kept in touch with them over the years. Duke is the true hero of our family his last act of kindness was the life he gave to these families.

When Duke died, something that concerned me most were the event that took place after his accidents. The kids he was with waited at least ten minutes to get help; they were afraid and panicked. None of them knew CPR or what to do in an emergency. I didn't ever want another parent to experience the pain our family had experienced when we lost Alex and Duke. I knew it was not in my power to keep everyone from pain, but I decided to make it my mission to do what I could. In 2011, a year after Duke's death, I started the Alex and Duke De Rego Foundation. The Foundation's mission was—and as is to this day—to empower young people in Hawaii with valuable water safety and emergency lifesaving knowledge, so tragedies like ours can be prevented.

We partnered with organizations like the Junior Lifeguard Program and Hawaii Rescue Tube Foundation. The vision has been to make our water safety and ocean awareness training part of every sixth-grade student's curriculum in the state of Hawaii; teaching them CPR and how to respond when emergencies arise. In doing so the foundation would be impacting thousands of lives and hundreds of communities in the Pacific and beyond. Wherever these kids go, for the rest of their lives, they will have this little piece of knowledge to potentially save their life and the lives of others.

Starting the foundation, for me, was a way to see Alex and Duke live on. Their tragedies did not have to be the end, their stories could impact children well into the future. While speaking at a church event in February of 2012 a lady attending the service—after hearing my story—gave me this scripture: Genesis 50:20, "You intended to harm me, but God intended it for good to accomplish what is now being done, the saving of many lives." (NIV)

Chapter 12:

A Broken Love Story

When I met Lamar on May 19, 1990, I had just come out of an abusive relationship that had lasted five years off and on. Lamar had moved to the Big Island from Oahu and was staying with a bartender friend I worked with. He was single, I was single, and the rest is history. He was the love of my life. He was handsome, had a funny sense of humor, was strong, and wasn't afraid of hard work. Not being afraid of hard work was a lesson he had learned working on the pig farm his family owned. With this work came a lot of physical pain, but Lamar also endured emotional pain at the hands of his father. I know this was something he never quite dealt with and I believe at times it left him emotionless; his way of not wanting to feel hurt or pain.

Lamar was a city boy by all accounts, his days were spent working hard and his nights were spent in the clubs in Waikiki. His father also owned a bar, so many nights you'd find him behind the bar serving up drinks. It wasn't unusually for him to show up on the farm in the morning having come straight from the clubs. He knew how to have a good time and enjoyed it. When I met Lamar, he was 33 years old, and I was 29. I remember being really surprised when I asked him if he had children and his response was "Yes, three daughters."

I had never dated a guy with kids. I was curious, though because he never spoke much about his daughter's the first year we were together. I sensed there was pain in their relationship. My family loved Lamar. He was liked by everyone, especially my favorite uncle Maitland Akau. It was my uncle who got Lamar a job when he moved to Waimea, a job that turned into a great career for him. He worked in construction and started out as a laborer, those were tough years. On the farm, he had been his own boss but now he had a boss telling him what to do.. Our weekends were filled with beaches, barbecues and alcohol. We spent many years partying on the weekends. This had been a lifestyle for Lamar before I met him, and I adapted to it.

Some individuals can find alcohol to be a great way to fill a void or empty dark hole inside of you; forget all your troubles. I knew Lamar was holding on to a lot of pain because I had spent many nights listening to his stories, regrets and hurts. I loved him and had compassion for him.

Pain did an absolute number on our relationship in more ways than one. Pain from the past, pain we caused each other and pain from the death of our sons. I cannot speak for Lamar, but I can understand his numbness at times throughout our 25-year marriage. I know people can change; I speak from experience. I came to a point where I realized certain habits and choices didn't serve the greater good in me and I wanted to make a change more than anything else.

Change looked much different for me and Lamar as a couple. In 2005, when Alex fell into the ocean, we stopped partying, drew closer to one another, and held tight. We seemed to stay that way until the mortgage crash in 2008. When I lost my job, this is when I first started feeling like I was on my own; alone.

The boys recognized how their father had disconnected and I always made excuses for him. Not wanting to accept that the love we once had for each other might have faded. Then, in 2009, when I was diagnosed with cancer, the intimacy between me and Lamar became non-existent. No woman wants to accept that the love of her life no longer feels the same. Despite the distance growing between us, I had to keep it together because I still had Dukie to care for. Duke had been my saving grace after losing Alex but then in 2010, he was gone.

With Duke's death, I watched Lamar become an empty shell of a man. He had suffered pain no parent should ever have to live through; twice and it was devasting. But I had suffered the same pain.

Instead of focusing on the pain I leaned into God all the more. I needed someone to comfort me through my pain, give me reassurance in my struggles, and encourage me in my lowest moments; God was there. He never left me.

In 2012, we separated and Lamar moved out of our home. Our divorce was not finalized until 2016. During the four-year period, life continued happening. I ended up losing my youngest brother Randy who, at 48 years old, lost his battle to pancreatic cancer. Another devasting loss in my life. Through it all God has blessed me with a wonderful family and friends who stood by my side with unconditional love and compassion. In every circumstance there was hope, and the love of the Father.

Romans 5: 3-5 says: "Not only so, but we also glory in our sufferings, because we know that suffering produces perseverance; perseverance, character; and character, hope. And hope does not put us to shame, because God's love has been poured out into our hearts through the Holy Spirit, who has been given to us." (NIV) As I close out this chapter, I want to speak to the women who have had to pick up the pieces in their family for one reason or another. Maybe financially, maybe emotionally, whatever it is. I understand there may also be men in this same kind of situation. I hope you can be encouraged by this chapter and certainly don't want to exclude you. However, I recognize I cannot, being a woman, speak specifically from a man's preceptive.

Whomever you are, you might feel as if the weight of the world is upon you. You may not even be sure if you can continue. I want to tell you there is hope.

I still have deep compassion for Lamar but something inside me had to accept I could not be his savior.

Chapter 13:

Life Goes On

*M*y son Kaleo was expected to be paralyzed. Although my life felt paused for a moment, everything around me continued. Thankfully Kaleo recovered. Alexander fell into the ocean. Once again, my whole world came to a standstill. My heart shattered into a million pieces but life around me continued on. I was diagnosed with breast cancer, Mommy passed away, Duke was involved in an accident—life changed forever in each of those moments but never stopped.

Why am I saying all this? Because life is full of many unexpected happenings. We can plan and prep as best we can but none of us can truly prepare for everything. If we are not careful, the weight of this reality can paralyze us from living.

If someone would have asked me when I was younger where I thought I might be today, I never would have guessed here. I never would have expected to have gone through all that I have gone through; yet I have and I'm still here by the grace of God.

Kaleo Gambill is an amazing son. He saw the person I was before I got saved—drinking, smoking, partying, and fighting with Lamar. That was the mom he knew and, in some ways, I felt I had failed my son; maybe my actions hindered his own faith.

When I got saved and began talking about Jesus changing my life, it made sense for him to be skeptic. He wanted to see if my actions aligned with my words, who could blame him? Then he went through his own struggle with guilt when we lost Alex. His boxing coach and mentor Gordon Fernandez Jr. helped him deal with his emotions.

In 2011, Kaleo held the amateur MMA 185lb BJ Penn Just Scrap Title. Then in 2012, Kaleo turned pro and signed a contract with Pro Elite MMA—fighting in New Zealand, Japan and Honolulu. He left the sport in 2014 to focus on his family. Kaleo holds a brown belt in Jiu Jitsu and trains under Ricardo Cavalcanti Jiu Jitsu. It keeps him focused and grounded. He has always been my son who pushed the limits. When he was told he couldn't do something he would prove you wrong; always strong-willed. I am so thankful to see the man he is today. Both he and Mahea have gone through many trials and have continued together, I am so proud of them. They live in Kawaihae on the Big Island of Hawaii. Kaleo owns and operates his own business and Mahea is a swimsuit designer and an avid water woman. They have one daughter, Hualilia'omalie, "Lili", who is truly a blessing.

Auwae De Rego is also a wonderful son. He was always away attending school when tragedy struck home which meant he would have to fly in and disrupt everything in his life to be with us. I know this was a lot for him to deal with. He always did what he needed to do for the family, coming home to support us, and never complained. He was always concerned about me and my feelings. I can still see the pain and uncertainty in his eyes every time he came home. He loves his family unconditionally and has always looked up to his older brother Kaleo, even though some people mistaken him for the oldest. Some of my favorite memories with Auwae were the times I attended his college football games at the University of Arizona. I can honestly say there is nothing like college football!

Today, he works fulltime as a longshore man; a job he pursued for eight years before he got it. One thing I can say about Auwae is that he sure is persistent. When he puts his mind to something, he goes after it. He is married to Hanalei Carter, a flight attendant and parttime realtor. Together they own and operator a small construction company, building and selling homes. They live in Kea'au on the Big Island of Hawaii and have one son Isaac, "Ikey", who is two years old.

Ululii Sansano is Lamar's youngest daughter. Although this makes her my stepdaughter, she is my daughter. I can't take credit for giving birth to her, but I can take some credit for the woman she is today; God-fearing and beautiful inside and out. She heard about her brother Alex falling into the ocean on the news, got on a plane and flew here to be with us. She wasn't even sure how she would make it down to the campsite when she arrived. She waited at the top road and jumped in the first truck headed down the mountain to be with all of us. When I had my surgeries, she was there and took care of me when her father didn't. Then with Duke's accident, when we could not get on a plane to fly out, Ululii went to the hospital. She stayed by Duke's side until Lamar and I arrived the next morning.

Like the boys, she too was suddenly faced with unmeasurable tragedy and loss. The year after we lost Alexander, Ululii lost her mom, Trina Huihui, to cancer. It has only been by the grace of God that Ululii continues her journey in life. God has a great plan for her, and I am so thankful and proud of the woman she has become and her heart to serve others. She is married to Robert Sansano and together they have three adult children Tiare McArthy, Terri Amina, Tevai Amina, two younger sons

Robert "Bubba" Sansano, Ryder Sansano and two grandsons Tayden and Jaxton-Riggs. Ululii and Rob live in Nanakuli on the Island of Oahu.

Kien Aveiro, my hanai son (adopted through love), has been a part of my family since the boys were small. He was always at our home, more so whenever Auwae came home from school—weekends, spring break, summer break, or Christmas break. Kien was always with us. When Alex fell into the ocean it brought us all so much closer. We had never experienced this kind of tragic loss. As young as Kien was at the time, he was right in the water with Lamar, Auwae and Kaleo diving and looking for Alex. This event changed us all. He spent more time with us every day. Then, when Duke died, I am sure it was like losing a younger brother to him. After this, he began calling me mom. Even my brother Randy's death had an effect on his life since Randy had been his basketball coach and mentor for many years.

Tragedy can either make you or break you. Kien has always chosen to be positive and give support; for this I am most proud of him. He is always pushing himself to be a better person and a better dad to Kobe Alexander his six-year-old son and he actually shows up to Church when I invite him! Kien works fulltime as a foreman on residential projects on the Kohala Coast. He holds the American National & Pan American Championship Jiu Jitsu titles in his weight class. He is a brown belt and trains out of Foundation Jiu Jitsu Gym in Kailua-Kona. He lives in Waimea on the Big Island with his son Kobe and his dog, Shaq.

In Hawaiian, ohana (family) is everything. For me, my ohana was always important. Ohana started with my mom and the example she lived, and it continues with me, my kids and grand-kids. My siblings and I we all lived with Mommy well into our twenties. I'm sure this is why I have always told the boys and

Ululii that as long as God provides a roof over my head, they will always have a place to sleep or a warm meal to eat. I have kept this promise on one or more occasions. I am happy they are all making lives of their own and I am proud of who they are today despite all our ohana has been through.

With the passing of Alex & Duke, I knew I had to do something to prevent this from happening to other families. While looking at an inflight magazine on an airplane, I read an article about the next generation of lifesavers, Junior Lifeguards. As I continued to read the article, I realized this was the something I was looking for. The mission of the Junior Lifeguard Program lined up with the values I had in mind—water safety, ocean awareness, first aid, leadership skills; getting the kids off the streets, helping them learn a skillset to safeguard their lives and the lives of others. On December 29th 2011 the Alex & Duke De Rego Foundation was given its 501©3 charitable recognition by the Internal Revenue Services and our public purpose was to provide water safety and ocean awareness to Hawaii youth. Not wanting to reinvent the wheel we partnered with Hawaii County Fire Departments Ocean Safety Division's Junior Lifeguard Program. The Foundation began supporting the Jr. Lifeguard program in every way that we could for the next six years.

In 2016, a private school in our town asked me if our Foundation would do a water safety event for their middle school students to close out their health and safety week. We jumped at the opportunity and put together a water safety and ocean awareness education program that we now implement for middle school students on Hawaii Island. God has opened many opportunities for us to save lives both in the natural and spiritual since most of the schools have a Q&A session after my presentation. I will never forget this one young man who asked me how in the world I managed to get through everything that had happened to me with losing my sons. Although I do not enter the schools with the intent to testify about my faith, moments like these create amazing opportunities to share my faith. I was able to tell him how I lean on God each day and he gives me the strength to press on.

The Alex & Duke De Rego Foundations water safety and ocean awareness education program has been a success as a larger number of children are able to participate in our program through a school environment. The mission of the Alex & Duke De Rego Foundation is to empower young people of Hawaii with valuable water safety and emergency lifesaving knowledge. We believe that even one life lost to unpreparedness near the ocean, or the lack of First Aid / CPR is one life too many.

I know Alex and Duke are smiling down on us. In their short time here on earth they are making a difference in the lives of other children. I see it on the faces of students who go through our program I am so proud of the legacy that is Alexander and Duke.

A few months after we lost Duke, I was asked to share my testimony at a women's church conference. Before the conference started as we sat in a small group praying for one another one of the special guests from the mainland asked me what I was going to be speaking about. I told her about losing Alex and Duke and how God was giving me strength. She looked straight into my eyes and said, "God has this word for you. Genesis 50:20 "You intended to harm me, but God intended it for good to accomplish what is now being done, the saving of many lives. (NIV)" Don't forget that!"

I never forgot that scripture, it is the basis of the Alex & Duke De Rego Foundation. Every time I begin to struggle, I turn back to that scripture and stand on it. What I have been through has not been for nothing; God, you have equipped me to save many live.

Chapter 14:

Pick Up Your Cross

I love being a mother with all my heart, that is the only thing I truly aspired to be, a mom. I wanted to be just like my mom, have a house full of kids and grandkids. I realize now that was God's plan for her, and his plan for me was her. I am the product of a praying mother; it is her prayers that God honored. Those prayers strengthened me when I was weak, guided me when I was lost, loved me when I could not love myself, and gave me peace in the darkest valley. This I know for sure; God heard the prayers of my mom for me and he fulfilled them.

Losing a child is one of the most unimaginable things to go through. I use to think people who didn't want to have kids were selfish; then I lost Alex and I understood. I can understand why some individuals turn to alcohol or drugs to fill the pain of loss. I could have done this, and the world would have said it was okay. They may have said, "Her pain is too great"

Or, "She needs something to take it away."

Or even, "Just let her be, she lost two sons."

But I couldn't do that, not to my Heavenly Father, I knew he had my sons in his loving arms; everything inside of me believed this. I know, without a doubt in my mind, I will see Alex and

Duke again one day, yet there are still days my heart aches in their absence.

Although we know there is a time to die this side of eternity, none of us wants it to come anytime soon. We want to live long joy-filled lives with everyone we love. We want to see our children graduate, marry, and create families of their own. My heart goes out to every parent who has been robbed of those opportunities with their children. I know how painful this reality is.

Throughout this entire journey, the Lord has been—my strength, my rock—my God in whom I trust. I will not say that I am anything special but what I will say is we serve a mighty God that loves each one of us so much; he has a purpose for our lives. We will never have answers to all the questions we have even though some might try to rationalize why things have happened.

What does all this mean for me? God is in control.

""For my thoughts are not your thoughts, neither are your ways my ways", declares the Lord. "As the heavens are higher than the earth, so are my ways higher than your ways and my thoughts than your thoughts"" Isaiah 55: 8-9 NIV

His ways are not my ways. There are so many things he has planned that my mind cannot even fathom what he has in store. I take comfort in believing and trusting that he was there with each of my boys as they took their last breaths. He has taken them to an eternal place of joy without any suffering. They are with God and there is nothing but love in his presence. Selfishly, I long to be with them but I know, since I am not yet there, I still have purpose here.

Many people have been touched by my story as I have spoken at churches and events. People gasp, they cry, they hold their own children a little tighter when they leave. Many people look at me in awe, "How is it that you get out of bed in the morning, Shirley? How can you even function after such great loss?"

Let me tell you, the fact that I am standing here today is not at all by my own strength but completely and entirely by the grace of God. The Lord sustains me each and every day, he gives me the strength to continue on until the day I will see Mommy, Alex, Dukie, and all my relatives who have gone before me. When that day comes, my heart will be filled with joy, don't shed a single tear for me only rejoice!

This scripture often comes to mind Luke 12:48, "To whom much is given, much will be required." I often think about what I will tell the Lord when he asks what I have done with the talents he has given me. He will want to know what I have said and done for the lives which have crossed my path. Did I share his son Jesus with them?

Allow me to share this precious gift with you that you may receive this same peace and joy into your own life, all you have to do is tell Jesus you believe in him and want to know him more. Really, it is that simple, no lie. Tell him about all the hurt and pain you've experienced in your own life. Ask him to forgive you for the hurt and pain you may have caused someone else or even your own self. He already knows but releasing it through your words will make space for him to fill you with his joy, love and peace. Invite him to be your Lord and Savior.

And the Lord said, "Have you considered my servant Shirley? This is my life.

CPSIA information can be obtained
at www.ICGtesting.com
Printed in the USA
LVHW051547030323
740787LV00001B/1